A list of your author's books
are attached in the back of this
book for your inspection.

Spiritual Transformation of the Fourth Millennium

Old Time Conventional Religion Is Fading
New time Spirituality Is on the Rise

Lloyd E. McIlveen

Order this book online at www.trafford.com
or email orders@trafford.com

Most Trafford titles are also available at major online book retailers.

Print information available on the last page.

ISBN: 978-1-4907-2877-3 (sc)
ISBN: 978-1-4907-2876-6 (e)

Trafford rev. 04/12/2016

North America & international
toll-free: 1 888 232 4444 (USA & Canada)
fax: 812 355 4082

The views on religious spirituality and belief are presented in these texts as a result of your author's personal studies, many experiences and observations in those areas for a multitude amount of years and are not primarily derived from any state or religious educational facility.

The views are written for the purpose of helping to expand one's mental scope in mankind's belief systems. Your author is a book writer on needed subjects. This one isn't written primarily for any purpose of crusading or promoting a cause of the described contents. The "cause" is automatically evolving with the passage of time. Only people who agree with this inevitability will adapt to these unfolding practices. Others may need more time. Eventually, everyone will adapt to the inevitability of profound spirituality within.

These views on spiritual beliefs and their changes are not meant to unfold in a form of organized exploitation for power and profit; only for what is naturally beneficial for the spiritually inclined or interested individuals who desire belief stability without contradiction, illusion, mystery or deception.

Preface

Get ready for a spiritual realization! This book is all about how people have existed in spiritual fantasy and deception for now going on thousands of years; maybe more since reliably historic records are rare. The Bible is helpful, but yields stories of fantasy, exaggeration and misguidance by many of its authors. There is an abundance of guesswork and ad-libbing attached to the religious past and its history. A big percentage of it all gets aired out in these texts.

There is nothing like boiling down fantasy and deception to get near the truth pertaining to what has been going on in religion and the spiritual aspect of it all.

The chapters unveil the controversies of religious evolution and the basis of religious contention while observing inevitable changes of conventional religion to self-actuated spirituality.

Flaws in conventional religion are articulated on and exposed for those who believe the system of religious guidance is perfect. The supposed spiritual leader of the universe is questioned for qualifications and other possible realities.

The usual, unusual and supernatural beliefs are brought into focus and elaborated on for any religious or basic spiritual value.

The question arises of how much religious and spiritual knowledge do we really have in wise and broad perspective other than the limits of what we were trained for from ancient books.

Mankind's discovery of God is somewhat, but rationally and humbly described.

A question here is why are there so many religions. Those questions and elaborations are in these texts.

Something everyone needs is a basis for being more of a spiritual believer and less of a conventionally religious believer. It's here. Why? It's due; way overdue.

There are many fallacies in conventional religion and that's one of many reasons for exposing them, their probabilities and possibilities.

The text explains about a religious transformation presently taking place into self-spirituality.

Unreal, real and creative spirituality is covered in the text along with preliminary hints how to handle them.

Something seldom discussed is spiritual ownership should one care to be in charge of his or her own destiny.

There are a few literal "bumps" on the road of religious and spiritual differences on the way to arrive at what may be best, better, status quo, not so good or worse for an individual in a world of spiritual belief.

These scripts are designed for stimulating and exercising options of the mind for the benefit of having control over the self or the detriment of allowing one to be controlled by influence from outside the self (religious promulgators and their controversial version of divine guidance).

Reading the "whole" book will add toward expanding perception of spiritual cognance and may help greatly in preventing mixed feelings in the area of spirituality and control of the mind.

The title of this book "Spiritual Transformation Of The Fourth Millennium" is about changes in religion and spirituality which has passed through human transformation periods for around four thousand years and is now continuing forward with those changes into a fifth millennium.

What is more dependable than change just as the universe has been doing forever?

This script of "Spiritual Transformation Of The Fourth Millennium" is "the" original in writing and concept by this author in the years of 2008 and 2009. Any other similarity or likeness of this original version intended for copying, publishing or selling may and/or will be considered an act of fraud and legal due diligence will be litigated through our United States justice system.

Good, sincere, honest and meaningful intentions and efforts are prime goals of this author in book writing any literature intended for advancing the cause of human decency, respect, compatibility and emotional/physical stability for all who desire those qualities. Those who abuse our recognized and established literature rules, laws and statutes must pay their dues accordingly.

Contents

Chapter 1

Controversial evolution of belief

Evolution of the human species is clearly written from scientific evidence dating back prior to the Stone Age combined with theoretical, logical and rational analyzation, not sheer belief.

Sufficient proof is available to conclude mankind lived somewhere in six figured years before religious history's stories of man's origin. Seven figured years are only speculated.

Science uses cadaver parts, math deduction, geological surveys, evolving factors, laboratory testing and other analysis for determining mankind origin. Religious researchers uses old scrolls, heresay, changed and revised stories in the Bible and sheer belief for analyzing without provable evidence.

Science doesn't really care who is right. They just gather data and record their findings. They don't campaign or advertize their findings for the glory of science because science has never been based primarily on belief or stories.

Religious institutions have constantly promoted their inherited dogma by preaching on exaggerated stories written sometimes hundreds of years after the incidents occurred. Those stories were obviously reinterpreted for dramatically literary effects. Growth became necessary for the cause, so they traveled and crusaded industriously throughout nations spreading the word of God representing their particular religious organization. They promoted their creed and practices through churches and other community gatherings. Now, they have extended through radio and worldwide television as though people needed a constant reminder to continue their religious believing and practices. Sure, it's constant income for many.

The scientific origin of man and the religious origin of man appear to exist in wide spaced conflict. One may be true which results in the other being false or there about. Making sense of it for knowing how to spiritually believe or even not believe, if it goes that far, is what needs to be addressed and understood much clearer by many more people, at least at the present time.

Why do scientific and religious views seem so different and difficult to choose when one hasn't chosen a side to believe? They cannot be evaluated for which one is better because they are not alike subjects. They have to be evaluated based on which one adds up to making more down to earth sense than the other one and not based on believing only.

One person may be more science inclined from family background, more science related subjects in school or employed in science research etc. and tend to be a little more evolutionary minded and biased in it.

Another person may have been raised with Quaker or Jewish beliefs which rarely bend and may understand the logic of the scientific evolutionary theory, but may influentially stay with the religious view of mankind's origin for reasons of security.

A third person may be one who has had education in several areas along with several adverse and wonderful experiences which usually gains more flexibility in several aspects concerning which way, which one and how to believe. That person may adapt to one side easier than the other.

Even a very young person without any special background who was allowed freedom to think and believe may be able to choose a side without conflicting torment through a clear and uncluttered mind as, for instance, institutional training.

Exposure to broad concepts in as many areas as possible as compared to limited and typical scope of thought allows flexibility in understanding what may seem difficult decisions to choose as with religion or science.

"Striving" to understand "both" sides in a broad view is what brings the understanding into clearer focus.

All educational programming, even what may seem as opposing views, stimulate more openness for more efficient analysis of what one may believe is applicable to and with reality. We all believe according to the way we were programmed until we change it or someone else does. Got it? Programming one's mind is profound and usually quite mindfully coherent.

The most controversial subject in the world is about what people believe. The most controversial subject about belief is about religious belief. That's why there is so much fuss and ado about it. People have been led to believe religion is constantly promoted and repeated because they must constantly pay religious homage to divine supremacy for what "He" has done, what "He" is doing and what "He" will do. They have been led to believe, without the homage and worshipping, the lack of it might cause the "Lord" to fade away, possibly get angry or maybe even reverse the well known redemption of sin that allows one into the providence of heaven. The possibility, in that case, could automatically be true as anything: No Homage; no Lord. No Lord; no belief in "Him." Then, we would be back to the beginning with no Lord and have to start all over with something to replace "Him." Who knows what "man" would do?

None of that makes much sense at all unless the individual is prone to be unbending in conventional religion and still believes those man-made contentions about God!

God of some kind, which isn't as man perceives that image may truly exist somehow, but not as a talking voice equal to that in a dramatic movie scene. That aspect of conventional religion is pure childhood fantasy as, unfortunately, is taught to them "before" they have any ability to rationalize.

A great many of us spiritual exercising people are slowly passing through a transformational era of time when our conventional manners of believing and practicing "are" changing regardless of what we see or hear. Most people are not totally engrossed in that reality because the changes are of an evolutionary nature. Many see it. Most probably do not! When it is more realized, the changes will be more obvious and adaptation to it will be acceptably normal in the same manner as most all cycling changes of life and substance. Spiritual fear won't even be noticed any more than the changes in fear are noticed in any other inevitably changing cycle.

Divine believers often ask nonbelievers, "What if there really "is" a God?" almost as a hedge toward being on the right side just in case. That doesn't sound like any kind of meaningful belief. This is the insecurity people have been living with for a long time. It isn't belief. It's manipulative speculation.

Manipulating with belief is counterproductive in believing. It keeps the real sense of believing downgraded. True, it does help maintain membership in conventional religion for the benefit of the cause, but it also prevents broad scoped consciousness for really knowing which way to believe other than just joining the crowd.

A helpful alternative to prevent becoming a victim of "just in case" mentality can be to purposely attend many different church meetings including any nonconventional, religious science and self-actuated facilities. Study the spirit within to gain more filtered out perception on which way to believe.

That will be a "creative" method of gathering more evaluated incentive for understanding the power of self-sustaining and self-motivating spirituality. That's part of the oncoming evolution of belief; doing it independently of institutionally influenced spirituality. The institutions can do it too; which many undoubtedly are. They may have their limits because of their associated institutional pressures, but as controversial as it may all seem, this evolving transformation of belief "is" here for everyone who wants it; bar none.

So far, there are no signs of fictitious or misleading stories of human sacrifices, martyrizing, capitalizing, brutalizing or other issues of desecrative reproach in individual activated spirituality. It's pure.

Most evolutionary issues are natural inevitabilities, not of revolutionary nature. Who would anyone fight? There are no borderlines involved and there is no ground to take over. Besides, if and when everyone cares to display their intelligence as compared to ignorance, their instinct and curiosity will prompt them into looking, listening, reading and generally inspecting this transformation period and discover a much more significant benefit in what the movement is shooting for which is developing our own independent spirituality.

This independence and individuality is not to isolate us from one another. It is to open us and let us be free from conventional religious domination based on fear and fantasy. Freedom to think, believe and be honest with no pesky guilt feelings or spiritual worries is what perpetuates these obviously needed changes which sometimes appear irreversible. There is no reason to revert to archaically outdated beliefs when we have access to no ending spiritual philosophy as our security and strength of the future within our own selves.

Chapter 2

The basis of contention

Conventional religion historically fades into the past as less rational and documented proof of their ever being "reason" for that type of worshipping let alone the actual devotion to it. However, there is enough evidence from that fading past to substantiate spiritual believing was active going on thousands of years before the Bible was written. That means the conventional view of believing in God as stated in the first book of the Bible wasn't the beginning of everything on earth and heaven. There were millions of years of ancient history prior to that time and untold time of the universe prior to that time.

People have made themselves become subservient, obsequious and devotedly submissive to a belief in a Supreme Being whether they had enough legitimate proof or not as long as there was a word declaring and validating an existence of that assumed power before, during and after the book of Genesis and was perpetuated by several names over a period of time. Included among some were Elohim, Jehovah. Yahweh, Allah and finally God. The term God seemed to rein more prevantly as time passed and has remained the universally accepted name representing a particular manner of spiritual believing now going on thousands of years.

Without those representive words, there would be nothing to reach out for and worship. Humans couldn't believe in anything without thinking in terms of words. Words form our beliefs. We read, write, talk and listen in word fashion. How very unstable and unmitigatingly inefficient can we be believing in something supernaturally spiritual?

Those men (not women in those earlier days of religion) didn't even have a qualified education let alone possess knowledge sufficient to understand and interpret an existence of a supposed maker and maintainer of the incomprehensible universe. That knowledge is inconceivable. Obviously, humans were never supplied with intelligence to handle feats of those unreasonable ranges. Saying space is limitless or forever is an easy guess for "any" intelligence! The smartest minds can also claim space doesn't end; it just moves around in a big circle and they are unable to extend or extrapolate on that. Incomparably more intelligence, to say the least, would be needed to extend our limited capacities with the wisest of living beings. "God" himself knows, if you will, but isn't telling us just like "He" isn't talking to us about anything else. That's a whole other subject of unanswered questions pertaining to why we are not being contacted by this, so far, hypothetical entity called

God other than what we have been taught from the Bible as though those texts were anymore valid than what is written here to say nothing of other books on God.

The same perceptive cognizance applies to, at least, understanding anything pertaining to a creator and/or maintainer of the universe, its contents and its occupants wherever and whenever.

Viewing these magnificent possibilities must be left open, however, because of the optimism where "anything" is possible. For instance, we are finally living in an era of time and place for either inheriting, more efficiently absorbing and developing intelligence to effectively analyze the established beliefs of the ancient past.

You say there were facts in those days attributing to the "truth?" Look at the red tape required in determining what is fact "these" days. Facts in those days were interpretingly nebulous. Authors in those days could easily and openly deceive the readers;

especially when the text was written "long" after it happened when records of so called witnesses were dead for sometime and most needed evidence was not inclusive other than heresay with exaggerated views. How can anyone believe that way?

Some of the stories of supernatural beliefs were written in dramatic efficacy to inspire conventional religious belief which was very impressively portrayed in the Bible. If those types of stories were told in this day of age, no one would believe them and yet the people of now believe those "old time" stories!

While the authors wrote the stories and the people continued to believe them, the publishers and lecturers capitalized on them as they are currently doing. They convinced the people they would be better off by going along with it all and it has continued its destined phases of belief practices.

Oh, it may be truly wonderful to live in our fantasy of heaven forever somehow, but again, it's only wishful believing. None of us have ever had any idea, other than imaginary, deceptive, biased or dramatically described versions told of any details pertaining to what "we" may be or do in that foreverness or even if there is any we in that foreverness at all.

We call ourselves "we" because there is something to look at, feel and touch etc. We have no way of imagining what our supposed "spirit" will be or do in a phase or "place" in that supposed foreverness. We only have an earthly alive identification. We do not identify with being dead; only in the sense of the loosely spread institutional indoctrination which is promoted to keep humans "in line" while living.

Every alive thing on Earth including mankind, animals, fish, birds, insects, virus, bacteria, trees, bushes to mention only a few lives for awhile and eventually dies. Everything living—dies. Sure, new roots and eggs etc. form and new life springs out, but the lived out lives are over. Who ever heard of all those things mentioned going to another place after death? Oh yes, many humans claim they will continue their lives after death somehow, but nothing is ever articulated on the foreverness of all other life and death than humans. Why? Only humans live their lives around wishful thinking, trained beliefs and unrealistic mind projection.

There is value to be considered in connecting our human lives to that of our animal counterparts. After all, we are "all" animals of one type or another. Why would we deserve special care after death anymore than animals or any other living things? Are we bigoted against them as though our God only considers "us" as being any good for extended life, whatever that might be? That doesn't sound like a "good" God; at least not like the one humans believe, pretend, hope, wish and pray for.

Let's make up our minds. Are we dead when we die or are we not dead when we die or are we alive when we die? After we died from being alive after we died, what unscrupulously, deceptive state or purgatorial existence must we pass through with or without our choice or approval? If we are alive somewhere there in the interim, we might be lucky enough to die a quiet and permanent death just worrying about staying alive after death.

We didn't ask to be born and we didn't ask or expect to die, so who do we think we are asking and expecting to somehow live again after dying? Everything lives and everything dies. That's it! There is no more! We don't even have a choice.

If a person is unbendingly convinced or chooses to believe living somehow continues after dying, that is truly a birthright privilege, but that person will be living in an unreal world of life in a spiritual aura of pure fantasy which, realistically, is a configuration of "nothing" unless it is creatively and materialistically applied in a stage play, a movie or described in literature form.

Respective of and to living and existing after death, there is only one way and it is definitely not a choice when one is alive. How one conducts oneself when alive has nothing to do with what happens after one dies. Nothing "happens" when one is dead. Anything which is possible to happen is only perceived by an alive being. Dead beings can no longer perceive and the whole universe no longer exists when one cannot perceive.

There is no reason, other than baseless fantasy taught by insecure, unrealistic and wishful thinking, for anyone or anything to "live" after dying. There never was and never will.

If one chooses to live life in a state of fantasy, there will be no "real" life to live. Maybe it's better to arrange life for its creativity, productivity and enjoyment as long as possible with the belief of whatever will happen will happen anyway regardless of how we believe and do or don't do; Maybe!

The term and/or belief in God fits in largely with our decisions to figure it all out or just go along with what others say in the respect of whether the "term" God is used or the "belief" in God is used. The "term" God is a word describing a type of belief explained in your Author's book, "What God is and isn't." Belief in God obviously speaks for itself and hopefully, after all angles of study and questioning from both views are considered, resolves in a self-satisfactory decision toward maintaining one's present manners of believing or engaging in a transformation to another plane of spiritual approach and belief. Next, there is the option of not choosing "any" form of spiritual belief at all even to the point of not believing in the self. The individual making that decision is the "only" one who is right for that person. That's part of the rawness of reality.

This is only the beginning of religious interrogation and analyzation.

Chapter 3

Observing inevitable change

Humans seem to have a dedicated, acquiescent and almost inherent desire to believe in something big and powerful whether it is real or not. Supernatural even "sounds" big and powerful. People would rather be drawn into it because they prefer to believe their lives and deaths will be better by sticking with it.

Churches, preachers and church goers are constant with their religious promoting. Why? They congregate once, twice and sometimes more times a week; every week throughout the years come hell or high water. They support the cause of a word that has a very strong tendency to regulate and even control the programmed, exploited and/ or deceived participators. Sure, that's a somewhat biased accusation of divine type power being socially and spiritually not fitting or maybe even not fair in a world of secure conscious establishments bent continuously toward convincing the people of their righteousness. After all, the more they convince the people a Supreme Being is real, the more "they" believe it and the more money is made. It's a very secure job. Why would they want to change it?

Actually, the churches, preachers and church goers are all participating and supporting mass deception among one another by not viewing another dimension of belief and spirituality.

Believing without questioning is not only mentally incompetent, it represents an obvious and inhibited frame of thinking which, in turn, restricts one or millions more from gaining more necessary and expansive knowledge for being intellectually and physically healthier and more readily adaptive to the rapid changes and many fluctuating conditions on this planet.

If surviving as well as possible for as long as possible on this fastly changing planet is high on the list of "living" priorities, then it's time to start branching out and realistically maturing and developing the self for adapting to the inevitable changes of old time anxiety and fear oriented dependency to a new self-sufficient spirituality of the future. Masses of religious, metaphysical and nonreligious people are in process of transforming and adapting to it without a lot of noise about it.

Living a life of being self-sufficiently healthy and secure while accepting an inevitable life's end of living beings does not run parallel with believing a supposed Supreme Being will guide every living being in the right direction all the time or even any of the time. All that happens in that area isn't necessarily what people want, expect or even pray for. Most of the good things desired are only what religious people "believe and hope" will happen without their applied effort and much of the time doesn't happen at all. There is more of a possibility these desired requests or expectations "will" happen when one prays or program's for something, then applies effort which supports odds to a favorable ratio for a more practical and reasonable outcome.

Directing a prayer to a believed higher power, whatever that may be, can be effective when one supplies effort in supporting the cause somehow. Directing those requests without willingness to be helpful in some manner is asking for something for nothing. That usually doesn't work. Prayers or programming to the self "does" work most of the time.

Many times when a person believes strongly with the desired request, that person will indirectly do little things which supports the cause thereby materializing its existence. One may call it responding to a prayer, but it may also be a result of contributing to the cause or just plain luck and that individual may give God the credit by saying, "Thank you God," when the credit would be more deserving to the self.

If a person depends on that kind of "luck" or skill of praying, there may be many disappointments ahead. Remember the saying, "God helps those who help themselves." That statement has basic merit for accepting responsibility for the self, but at the same time cancels the belief and theory where "God" is directing everything. Those are all strictly human thoughts and contentions. Everything believed or said to be directed or handled by God, if you will, tends to be insightful, invented, conspired, contrived or just plain made-up by ordinary human thinking, not thinking as though "God" was directing it.

Most thinking processes are pure guessing; "I think I can do it." "I think it will rain." "I think this plan will work." "I think she is meant for me." It's all guesswork. That's all we have.

Sure, we can say, "God is real, but that's only stated. That doesn't "make" it real. That only makes it believed. The belief is only a spiritual or psychological thought which has no molecular substance to it and occupies no space whatsoever. Hence, it doesn't exist, so how can anyone believe in anything that doesn't exist? The answer to that is easy. People are "led" by people who manipulate through the process of indoctrination and they may very likely be victims of the indoctrination themselves. That's where the conjured up beliefs of a supposed God has probably or as much as inadvertently strayed from earlier mankind's spiritual innocence and purity to an evolving man-made "obey the rules or else" conglomeration of a whole flock of secondary leaders who supported a very mysterious, silent, unseen and unknown leader incognito they eventually attached a name to.

If the concept (because everything thought of is a concept) of God is a valid and more provable reality than not, that entity would be inconceivably more intelligent than puny little humans to say the very least and certainly wouldn't relate to us on "our" level of intellect. Proof of that is also simple:

If that entity we have named God was or is real like we perceive the term real and "he", if you will, decided to communicate with we humans, "he" probably wouldn't pick on one, two or three humans to talk to at different times or different places as indicated in religious scriptures. "He" would probably exist in our consciousness without having to actually "speak" to us like an ordinary human. All that business of God speaking to a human is human thought and fantasy which only exists in Biblical stories and religious movies. Also, the terms He, Supreme Being, God and the like probably wouldn't exist if they were naturally inherent.

If "all" living beings truly exist as being relatives somehow, why is there such an enormous spiritual/ Godly support for humans only? Are we all that prejudiced to our own relatives? Do we really believe any all powerful entity of "God" only cares to deal with humans separately from all other life in our solar system or anywhere else? Those who think and believe in that elementary and narrow scoped manner certainly cannot be followers or supporters of "any" belief which supposedly has claim to or maintains such an inconceivably broad spectrimed area as everything in the universe plus whatever is on the other side etc., etc., etc.

Now, all the talk about what God has said to humans was supposedly said thousands of years ago. Why then? Why not thousands of years prior to that time or why not now or in the future?

The belief in God as a man or something similar began when mankind's population began to grow and presented problems of possessions, then greed, then power plays to dominate; all coupled with hostility, mistrust of all the states of lower consciousness which caused mankind to torture, enslave and kill one another. Something was needed to alter that fearful and desperately cruel way of life. There was no one decent at the top to control. A few people envisioned a giant father of some kind was needed to direct humanity from drifting themselves into a chaotic future, but they only possessed desire, fantasy and dreams to produce that giant. That's how it all began.

Low and behold, that giant father was discovered for the solution in civilizing mankind. Sure, it took a long time to organize, develop and become more powerful than the way they were. Organized religion was due. That need caused a mind factor of fear, peace and solace all at one time they could structurally depend on more than their existing insecurities. It wasn't perfect, but they believed it was better than what they had.

Believing in something that incredibly huge passed through many stages of growth before coming together with so many people. It wasn't sudden.

Many religious contradicting battles of different natures were emanated in that growth process even up to the present time.

The philosophy and belief of a Supreme Being did wonders in helping to civilize people who "could" be civilized and conform to be led by a "supposedly" peaceful entity with "His" followers and supporters; which was only a belief propagated by the incessantly strong and craving desire to maintain peace among men. That required cooperation with one another coupled with time acquired rules, patience and spiritual guidance by those many people who allowed themselves to be religiously indoctrinated with very cleverly induced rules for peaceful and honorary redemption which would supposedly lead to living infinitely while feeling even better about voluntarily supporting that cause. Many others had no choice and remained in detained religious conformity through incarceration, slavery political conquests, hostilities of war, social and family expectations and many more covert and forced influences. Many of those people were denied or shuned certain rights to sort out or analyze alternatives, substitutes, truth validity, possible deceptive education or even plain right or wrong in exchange for the more simplistic manner of judging spirituality which was burdened with inaccuracies and narrow scope views. If they were lucky, they settled for the least as do so very many people this day of age.

We are constantly learning more about the necessity of knowing more about anything before accepting it. Religion is no exception and that goes for any messianic apparition too. That resolution can be a key factor in judging for a final decision in determining the value of divine intervention, exchange, belief, worship, practice or dependency.

Sure, the value of all those religious exercises may be acutely and applicably utilized everyday in any nondeceptive and open for scrutiny belief "whatever" they may be. Let's view them all.

"All" mankind's spiritual beliefs have flaws; some little and some gargantuous. Why? They are beliefs evoked by man, not the figure referred to as God. Reference to and in God in this book is stated and meant to be understood as the term or word, not as an actual or absolute entity.

This book is also not presented for defining or condemning a belief in divine influence. It is presented as a gesture to see or acknowledge another manner of spiritual perception; especially when, in all man's attempts to shore up and/or change conventional beliefs and contentions, there are obvious indications of ineffective, contradicting and outdated basis for further preserving a fading institution referred to here as conventional religion in general which covers all God indoctrination.

Spirituality is great. It's here to stay. It's flexible. It's open for exchange of dialogue. It's open for mutual change. It's not guided by stringently disciplined rules which, many times, causes more trouble than they are worth. We now have needs to escape narrow and restrictive rules that prevents growth in and with larger amounts of people. We need more openness to broaden people's scope for this new world we are entering into. If we truly want peace among us, we must not expand our resources for dominating and escaping reality by one or more Gods who are not really in touch with us. At least we have no knowledge of that other than the insufficient evidence available. Religious interpretation has no evidential value; only more of the same deceptive mind enslavement and institutional security of which is overdue for change.

Chapter 4

Changing concepts concerning conventional religion

God may be. Your author, among billions of other people over time, have just needed more proof. Believing only is not enough. What people have conjured up about God isn't anywhere near enough to believe in when it comes to anything as enormous as that possibility. It's asking for more than could ever be possible. Adapting to it because it seems easily believed is the same as maintaining and retaining vulnerability to suggestion which results in brain washing effects.

A person's word or a person's belief from being conventionally indoctrinated is not enough.

Experiences believed to be a result of praying is not near enough.

The fact this divine worshipping has continued for thousands of years isn't proof at all. It must be objectively resolved.

Just because hundreds or thousands of people congregate to hear what mankind says is God's word, the history of God or God's guidance still isn't enough to conform to the conventional manner of spirituality. There is much more to be learned.

The rules of conventional religion were "all" written by men. Once again and many times as time passes; only by men. Women never had a choice to contribute toward the cause; only men which is contradictive to the Godly contention of loving, sharing and having respect for one another. Even Jesus taught a form of equality and fairness as he hoped it would be among "all" people. Adversely speaking, he surely didn't encourage the men to promote prejudicial domination over women. One would think he could for a man who was taught from birth to believe he was more a part of God than any other man, but wasn't really capable of doing a lot more than any other man except for his glorious abilities to preach. That was a significant flaw in religious propagation. Man's domination over women actually began much further back than man's creation (invention) of God according to what has been gathered from the theory and research of evolution. Evolution reaches back hundreds of millions of years, if not longer and "God" only appeared recently when mankind started talking about "Him." That's the way it appears.

Why has conventional religion grown so big as the millenniums pass? People of those past millenniums and also today had to and still do follow anything that appears to offer them something more than what they have. This pertains particularly to small children. They may be lucky enough to have a mother "and" a father. The parents were raised the way their parents were with holy influence and they tell the children there is something bigger. The children follow what the parents do. The children's beliefs become profoundly vested and they pass it on downline almost like robots.

The Bible was and still is full of detectable flaws and why? It was written by people, not any god. As unskillfully as it was written, people have been gullible enough to believe everything it says as being the truth. This is where interrogation of as many other areas of spirituality and nonreligious presentations of as many as possible will increase with much more cognizant perception and perspective for determining what may be true and what may not be true. Without that effort put forth, one will not be close to the truth because truth in religion and spirituality is only in how close one can get to touch, feel, hear, see and smell it. Understanding helps too. It all adds up. Doing little won't help with getting the truth. More on truth in later chapters.

The child doesn't dare vary from the rules for "fear" of punishment from God. No one wants punishment and they are led to believe in heaven almost like it's a reward for being good. Is that a manipulation or is it an outright lie? Talk about brain washing. The child becomes hooked. He or she cannot believe any other way after that. That is spiritually unfair. Many of the little kids barely know, if any at all, what death is and yet they teach them about heaven which is something they nor anyone else can comprehend. How absurd!

Even when that child reaches adulthood, his or her attitude supports defending anything supporting the "established" beliefs. They will defend it with whatever it takes; even with hostile or denial dialogue, parting of the ways or even organized fighting which occurs in various forms as we know.

First they are trained to believe God is good and peaceful. Later, they discover God chooses sides in war as seems to be the mentality of opposing countries in the mid-east at this time if not in many other times. How ignorantly contradictive religious training and belief can be. They continue to root for their own country in battle as though God has nothing to do with the other country. That defeats the purpose of being religious in "any" way shape or form. It is massive power playing with people's minds so they will live by their institutionally established rules and not attempt to rationalize anything more into it or out of it.

Can you imagine giving up all those covert and deceptively acquired rules of any or all the conventional religions and becoming a person of basically good, pure and peaceful intentions with cooperative practices; a person who would be as good if not better in purity than a God living person with all the rules?

Can you imagine living a life of a good, respectful and decent person without suffering guilt, fear and anguish of being penalized somehow everytime you turn around?

The material in this book isn't meant for telling anyone exactly what to do. It's meant for submitting views of what people have trapped themselves into which are very hard to change and that has been the objectives of all the religious manipulators for sweeping everyone as possible into the realm of mass control. That control can only be surmised as having been initiated millenniums ago for keeping people domestically civil and easier to handle in massive amounts by convincing them God may punish them or reward them after death etc., etc. only with the conditions of conforming to the rules.

We have been noticing, in more recent eras of time, the philosophy of religion has been transforming from maintaining subordinate rules of worship and purity to being entertained more in church with more stimulating music, singing, comedy and what may be termed as more interesting activities of various natures. Why? This keeps people mesmerized in their deceptively peaceful religious state of unreal "or" false security.

Yes, that's what conventional religion in spiritually free countries are having to do to retain their memberships. Loud musical bands, food, parties and more activities other than religion is the way of average church life now which "does" require more money on an ongoing basis. Guess where it comes from. It comes primarily from the membership who seem to perpetuate it all in this confusing time of religious contradictions between old time believing and believing of the future.

Jesus made a big issue out of not capitalizing on goods for sale on spiritual property. He wanted that manner of spiritual respect to continue into the future. Where has it gone? We see it now:

There are more churches having thrift sales as time passes for the sole purpose of making more money. Along with it all, there is less respect, less friendliness and less sincerely caring for anyone other than with whomever they already know in religious centers and congregations than history documents. That is contradictory and not socially spiritual as originally intended. This is simply saying people "do" want a master to take care of them, but the rituals for that service must now be inspiringly entertaining. Religion wasn't originally meant to be a flashy and noisy spectacle. It was meant to be a quiet and peaceful time of nurturing and honoring an inner spirit with whatever outer spirit one would choose. Now we are beginning to transform in a manner of our educated choice.

Money, fun and the security of getting something for as little effort as possible has been creeping into our spiritual communities around the world and are not only creating an alienation of pure, innocent, indisputable and indissoluble religion, whichever they choose, but the inevitabilities of their changes are now quite rapidly moving from those old time holy type beliefs to industrial, mechanical, technological, medical, comical, musical and many other 'cals replacing the needs of anciently structured spirituality.

Things "are" changing in worldwide religion. Remaining in archaic deception doesn't favor anyone anymore; only fools them.

There may be a time when we may all revert to maybe "both" conventional and independent spirituality while ingratiating our particular manner of believing or worshipping. It apparently is not now!

Because of obvious deterioration of the artificially established conventional religions and their manners of disseminating spiritual indoctrination for millenniums, the people being set as they may seem are slowly making changes in the conventionally controlled area of artificially designed divine influence.

Spiritual existence is real without a "Him" in charge and has inherently casy access for everyone who "is" in charge of their brain. Conventional religion, as compared to pure spirituality, theoretically assumes more institutional influence over anyone submitting to their beliefs. Our brains are meant to make "all" our choices which includes that of our beliefs. This is our natural birthright freedom regardless of any right restricting regime one may live under.

Living, practicing and worshipping in, alongside or under conventional religion is a surrendered state of mind to that cause which is subjective of strict man-made rules restricting "complete" freedom to think, speak or practice anything other than what the instigators originated. Extensive research, at least equal to the very strong, relentless and ongoing contentions of conventional religion has revealed whenever statements were made supposedly by God, the voices had to converge in the mind from the conscious area to the subconscious receptor of mind therefore producing an image in the beholder's brain believed to be received exteriorly. This is typical of anyone who had or does have emotional pressures bearing on their emotional stability that creates a neural connection from stored thoughts to rational desires and wishes thereby resulting usually in subliminal incoherent voices, not clear-cut voices. However, the mind can imagine what the voice says depending on what direction the individual's desires may be headed. As anything else, there is no absolute resolution to this analysis of reality versus illusionary fantasy. Each one of us creates truth.

The stories of miraculous nature in the Bible as well as any religious stories were published with many uncontested flaws and the writers loved the glory and freedom to interpret their own versions of truth.

Whoever questioned whether a story in the Bible was true or not? Authors simulated acts of nature, people and supposed Messiahs who also simulated very well in their roles. Many really believed them.

Many copied them. Many deceivingly acted their different roles. Many had to lead. Many needed glory and most just followed along not really knowing too much except to keep their noses clean and they would ascend to a forever land somehow of which they never had a clue of either.

No one has ever had even a small clue of what heaven would amount to other than what was written in Hebrew scrolls or verbally passed mostly through Judaistic versions of belief. This was a grappling period of time when religion of God was being tossed around like eggs in a frying pan. Almost everything conjured to believe in was akin to wild guessing, but they had to establish rules for everyone to follow which would substantiate and strictly maintain the original form of "rule of law."

The rules of law in those days certainly weren't very liberal. Actually, they were quite narrow in scope and almost sadistically cruel with the belief it would keep people domestically "in line" with religiously established destiny. One example was the religious condemnation of anything believed or practiced outside or other than the conventionally established realm of divine power or control. Another example is where penalties for committing blasphemy ranged very narrowly from life isolation to immediate death.

Those examples alone are enough to show the wild and narrow minded mentality and mannerisms of those early times where the goodness and peacefulness of God was supposed to be the order of the day; each day, not just whenever they wanted it.

Most all conventional literature's rules and follow-ups were based from those earlier times of unsubstantially acquired creed, guidance, beliefs and other mind twisting actualities.

We are now beginning to notice and daringly put into exposing religious treatise for more meaningfully and acceptable creed and legitimately analyzed spirituality for guidance in real actualities we can weave into on or around our present sphere of spiritual capabilities.

When we ease off on these archaic and restricting rules meant for ancient communities, we see spiritual perspective has limitless possibilities which eliminates cleverly, but faulty beliefs of the narrowly indoctrinated people of the past. With that new freedom, we see living this life around purely developed fantasy for a forever becomes psychologically unnecessary. When we finally realize no one has ever done it other than what someone may have rumored, then we are all in the same boat, so to speak and the only necessity there ever was for heaven was because someone said it was there. If the subject was never raised, there would be no desire for it just like all other nonlanguage and nonrationalizing beings.

Dreams for being successful in life are valid states of mind because we've seen it happen and we can realistically make it happen. Fantasies derived for reasons of insecurity, greed of more, fear of being miserable and the like is burning energy in a completely wasteful and unnecessary manner.

Remember, what "is"—"is" and cannot be changed when it pertains to death regardless of how one has been trained to believe. It's been going on for a very long time and undoubtedly hasn't changed a bit. That doesn't make death bad or not enough life anymore than life after death might be too long. It just makes it what it "is." The only change in the whole scenario is what one "thinks" it is when we are alive.

When we die, which means our whole body and brain, our individual spirit turns off too. The lifetime energy in a dead person ended permanently and doesn't return. Anything counter to that has no logical basis for dialogue except wishful thinking, hoping, stubborn clinging and inability to accept reality which is more provable now than ever.

We humans have a tendency to think there is something wrong, negative or fearful about death.

If there is something wrong with it, there must be something wrong with being born. If there is something wrong with both, it seems logical to say judging birth or death has no value except for what mankind had invented. That, of course, is only a way of viewing it and that's all we have for understanding, tolerating, figuring and believing. It's what we conjure up in our minds or—are led to believe.

Continuing with after death living, since we only identify with our present body and mind existence and have no idea at all what "may" exist on the "other side," if you will, how can we have a desire, a need or maybe even an instinctual tendency to "just" exist somehow without our body and mind? Even imagining that for the rest of eternity could be mind boggling let alone actually existing in such a state where there is nothing to think with. See, it's already getting a little irritating just touching the surface of it all.

There is no reason for "going" beyond life. Preconceived ideas about the so called joys of heaven are just that. There is no reason for "going" anywhere except for what is conjured up by humans. Reality is what "is," not what is fantasized or conventionally "learned."

There isn't enough emphasis applied to what is "learned" particularly in spiritual areas of life. People can learn anything and become righteously "hooked" on it. If it's spirituality, it would be great if the learned spirituality would be fitting and updated to the present time. That's each person's responsibility to "seek out" that important manner of believing in as many ways as possible. This is only one of them. More will unfold as time passes. We can depend on that.

Chapter 5

Facing spiritual change

All conventional literature, its religious preaching and their doctrinal beliefs may have fed mankind's fearful consciousness for thousands of years without much interruption and seems to be maintaining that continuity without being openly scrutinized mostly due to unenthusiastic indifference, irresistible habit, fear of social or religious scorn, inflexibility and fear of being excommunicated, persecuted or somehow obliterated and whatever else imagined.

We are entering into a very complicated time of massive change on planet Earth. The strong and realistically educated people of this planet will survive quite well. The people who remain in unrealistic frames of mind and beliefs such as allowing one's destiny to be guided by an unknown Supreme Being will wither to the wayside unless they adapt with fluctuating and changing spiritual activity and beliefs. They have been traditionally following "ancient" structure and rules orientation based on fantasy; anxiety, fear and dependence, not on methods of self-security which are gaining momentum in philosophy, psychology and in individually nourished consciousness. These methods build nondependent strengths for survival and much more comfortably terminal acceptance.

All changes in the universe, on planet Earth as anywhere else "and" in the consciousness of all living beings cycle from one stage to another; even beliefs and adaptations to, as always, inevitable change with no exceptions. That's reality.

We are able to estimate time cycles of physical substance and social progress to reasonable degrees. Belief cycles happen as we record them and are only viewed from the limited past we know of. Stages of human beliefs have recorded much of that limited history, but estimating their future is somewhat unpredictable. All we know about the future of our spiritual type beliefs, so far, is how we have grown steadily throughout our history and are revealing signs of reaching a peak in dogmatic conflict and restlessness for change. Along with that, we can expound from our past and formulate with new consciously formed intelligence for estimating changes from indications of how mankind may be "willing" to make changes. That can happen with eventual enthusiasm to stimulate desire "for" not only adapting to overdue change, but to promote the learned and obvious necessity of expanding with these needed changes.

When one looks, one can see oodles of flaws in conventionally spiritual believing. If one doesn't look, one may miss them and remain aloof on belief progress.

Odds favor we are somewhere in the process of reaching a turning point of conventional believing and are headed away toward new opportunities concerning updated beliefs which fall into categories of their inevitable change. Evidence of rock hard origin indicates these changes will be somewhat slow due to the very set in their ways policies of institutionally organized religion and many of their committed followers.

How the progress of these manners of believing will occur depends on the level of logical intelligence acquired as time passes for people of all natures and/ or denominations to evaluate inevitable needs of change in increasingly large amounts of those people. More dominating institutional indoctrination for the cause of change may hinder and inhibit the open and free nature of self-spiritual dependency as compared to the customary visions of the ancient past.

Conventionally religious believing is, generally, the manner of worshipping which has been centrally accepted around the globe through religiously organized institutions in the past very few thousands of years. Prior to that era of time, most of what we refer to as religion was widely and sporadically spaced which means the time hadn't yet reached a point where all people around the world would come to an agreement of one God for all. Wasn't that big of us to let God know that; assuming there was a God. There were many scattered tribes with their own versions of what they worshipped, chanted or danced to. Religions in more civilized areas many times were institutionalized through monarchal control or other demagogical leaders who appealed to emotionally driven people. Changes had to be made then too.

Changing a political party can be tough to do because of ego pressing possibilities of being wrong in particular at voting time. Changing an attitude may also linger as resisting simply because someone else said it was bad. Changing jobs may have its benefits in time, but the transition may be initially awkward because of suddenly having to deal with many new people. Having a need to change soul mates may also be a very trying time because of inability to change vested habits with one another.

However, spiritual believing habits; especially the institutionally "trained" type, may be the most difficult habits to break even when indications of change may seem disturbingly due.

Almost no one, except very young people, will easily make changes unless the changes offer better opportunity, more money, a chance to overcome pains and miseries of physical and/or emotional distresses or be engaged with some form of glory receiving activity. How about just wanting to adapt with unfolding knowledge?

That last example may be why so many people remain mesmerized as part of what they believe is the foregoing conclusion to and with all actions and reactions on Earth. That's pretty big! Big and broad as that perspective may seem, the scope of believing on Earth is only a drop in the sea when compared to the immense mind expansion possibilities available of, with and in the no end space of what we refer to as our universe, we can very easily extend those possibilities so wide as to say the universe is within another universe and still another one yet. Going that far out, can we still say it is ours? We "can" stretch our thoughts.

It's a pretty deplorable and very elementary thought to believe present manners of spiritual believing is limited as the way it is at present to the way it will just barely exist into the vast concepts of change as future unfolds.

Entering into a time of vast change while depending on a believed in only Supreme Being without substantiation of its existence is very much like depending on pure luck. That does happen on a typically average basis of time whether skills are applied or not, but in the everyday and over all picture, that will only happen occasionally. We use our acquired skills to get reasonably good results more than we give ourselves credit for and put a great amount of effort believing an outside of body spirit is doing it. That's what needs more interrogating to arrive at changing the power of believing from supposedly outside the body assistance or control which is only speculated or imagined to the power of self-control "over" the self within. That's why we genetically inherited our brain which we must give credit to in building mankind's constantly increasing intellect for endless wonders of progress. Animals didn't do it. "We" promoted our growth and "we" know it! It's all in how one chooses to interpret the wonders of progress; especially in this case of alternative spirituality or growing out of conventionally motivated religion.

Now we are learning more how to be self-sustaining, get off our past dependency of a very old system of spiritual believing and inevitably rise above past errors of judgments and blend into new cycles of change. They are here facing us all.

We will automatically become stronger in every way when we conquer our need to be carried through life by a divine guiding light which is only a belief. The conventional aspect of that light "is" transforming slowly from the ancient borrowed power referred to as the noun God to oncoming spiritual power within our human species. "We" are gaining power over ourselves.

Eventually, all of us who will be living will understand more about spiritual power within running the show of life and less dependence of a hypothetical "leader" of the universe. Along with that awareness will be more education of how nature is connected with all movement and inevitabilities on planet Earth and elsewhere too.

Anything worth changing is conducive to supporting its inevitability. Mankind's desperate attempts to maintain control of conventional religion is weakening in spite of the money they spend on bolstering their efforts of creating new enthusiasm, incentive or penalties of which they obviously believe will promote continued religious detainment of their time consumed development.

Specific beliefs were undoubtedly at the crux of developing conventional religion originally in those earlier stages when many people did resist reasoning for those beliefs and still do.

Now, after millenniums of divine worshipping, forensic interrogation and insufficient resolution for validating their claims of absolute truth; conventional religion is steadily losing its religious credibility due to inflexibility of bending and blending with inherent spirituality. The old well known philosophy of everything that goes around, comes around applies in this message where spirituality "is" within and is due to be exercised by the self in our rotating time phase of spiritual believing.

Mankind, living with one manner of belief dependency or another, becomes subjected to new adaptations with the passage of time. If mankind ceases to grow in that evolving direction, their purposes will fade and only return in another reevaluated cycle of time if and or when mankind reaches that destiny.

The material in this part of the overall text is projected to necessitate awareness that conventionally directed religion of the ancient past creeping into our present time will no longer continuously and effectively serve the needs of our higher paced societies of mankind. We are now noticing changes.

The spiritual dependency of the past has served its purpose in the stages of spiritual progress and will fade with time. Names and titles will be much less needed with spiritual focusing becoming more prevalent within our own selves.

We must now be more assertively engaged in continuing to pioneer the individually practiced development of spiritual leadership within for our up and coming spiritual strengths and viabilities with methods relieving many archaically stringent rules only needed in past eras of spiritual evolution.

Eventually, with the rotating cycles of change and interchange, people who are inflexible to these changes may not experience the freedom and independence from unwavering religious rules, dogma and other inhibiting biases or which may occur in high level positions as spiritual freedom condemnation. Everyone must become aware if that becomes the order of the day, it will not only be counterproductive to any declining archaic beliefs; it will also temporarily inhibit the tendencies of natural and needed cycles of spiritual change to occur.

Realistically speaking, no one or organization can significantly stop or reverse the forces of inevitable change; especially when the momentum has already, but not seriously, been viewed. The people of the new way know it "is" moving forward.

Chapter 6

Flaw exposure through simple deduction

Probably the most widely accepted spiritual believing in more recent centuries of time has been, since there are no concrete facts, an imaginable figure of the term God depicted originally in mind's eye belief form and later in head and/or statue form where they could more materially and psychologically connect with their images through different Godly forms representing their beliefs. Finally, ahead in time, their inevitable changing views of spiritual connection meandered from material ritualism to the more mystic type spiritual worshipping which allowed them to worship or pray at random anywhere any time which led and spread to conventional religion of one invisible and indivisible figure represented by the term "divine" entity and a few other titles.

From those days of human conjured religion through institutional promotion, the "word of God" became rule of law among religiously joining nations and was also subjected to controversial hesitancy, disbelief, doubt, curiosity, debate and fear; especially when coupled with ritualistic ideas, beliefs and other lingering suspicion.

All those mixed feelings and lingering anxieties have proportionally led to increasing conventionally religious interrogation by more people than ever in quest of where alternating spiritual concepts may all lead and are now forming to a much clearer picture of long term learning, adapting, changing and repeating over and over through destiny "of" time and its change. We humans are only subjects to resist or flow along with the little known spiritual leadership which has been humanely invented and promoted from three to four thousand years. Now we are transforming from outdated believing to the self-sustaining new manner of believing within.

Relative to what may be real, nonexistent, actually happened or what "may" happen, we now have many curious aspects and faults to explore with the concept of God becoming susceptible to faltering or fading in its few thousand years of wondrously cycling influence. The following are flaws in conventional religion:

God is supposed to be good, right? According to conventional religion, we are supposed to be images of that God. How can we believe that when no one has ever seen that God? Everyone in current history seems to agree there is only one God now! That means if we could see that God, there would be only one look of a head, arms legs and body if that God is a he or a person like most God believers have indicated or even claimed. That is a ridiculous, immature and elementary manner of contending per se. Be that as it may, the billions of people who live on this planet all look different. How could all different people have the same image of "Him." That's a flaw.

If "He" is so good, why does He keep contributing more kids to the world to make us all more miserable in the overall picture? Overpopulation is ruining us! This is assuming, of course, "He" is in charge of everything. That's a flaw.

If "He" is so gloriously wonderful and realistically magical, why does he allow the goodness placed in us to do so incredibly many bad things like fighting, killing and torturing each other as much as we sadistically can? "He" could change that or anything else; that is, if "He" is truly so supernatural and magical as the originators planned or the supporters like to believe "He" would guide us. Flaws are there.

People cling to religious beliefs supporting divine influence. Why? Divine influence has kept those people mesmerized with the belief they were being continuously protected in everything they did during life and after death. They have seemed normal, but normal thinking people evaluate with common sense and reliable supporting evidence. If all worked out well, they were lucky which, as previously mentioned, can be an ordinary destiny; not controlled by divine influence. This is an example of conventional believing and "can" be helpful in reducing effects of fear. However, one must realize fear may also trigger a movement of self-protection at the right time. This takes the chance and any possible risk out of a negative situation. "God" may not always be there. Flaws may be seen in that scenario.

If there was a God everywhere all the time and was constantly interested in our well being, that would be great. We could get help fast from a quick and magical entity. We might even get a good word from "Him" too. That's going a little too far with believing, but so many people do go "all" the way with religious fantasy and won't budge in their set fantasies.

Most conventional religions teach how to believe in God. The student learns what is taught. It's nothing new. It's all very very old. "Everything" has been updated and improved in most societies of the world except conventional religion.

The question always lingers of whether or not "God" is in charge of everything, part of everything or not in charge of anything. Whoever explains it all is "only" guessing from heresay or what was read out of a book. That's a flaw.

If "God" is what makes everything happen everywhere, then mankind and all other living beings and things have no selective choices to do anything. That doesn't add up because we were all given a brain to plan our destiny with our brain, rationalize our decisions with our brain and exercise endless movements etc. with our brain. How can we rationalize "God" doing some of it and we do the other? That's only a wild human guess which would probably have different interpretations from one person to the next. That's a flaw as is with so many other claims and assumptions concerning God, what God supposedly "says" and what God does or doesn't do.

People have a natural and birthright choice to believe one way or another even if they live under strict penalty issuing control of which they became victims of, didn't resist and still don't know they became victims of those regimes. They are easily led to religiously conform regardless of dogma or creed. That is a totally unfair flaw.

Human's involved in conventional religion are inhibitedly involved as a result of not freely checking out philosophy, science and many spiritual alternatives first. They usually become quickly programmed into a particular religious study that sucks them into beliefs they become easily and happily willing to support. This happens in the cycle of conventional religion where life after death is deceivingly emphasized. That creed and practice of it stimulates further neurotic needs which, in turn, becomes a deceivingly secure, but at the same time, addictive way of life. This is an underhanded manner of adding another brain washed and paying member to the accumulating clan of organized religion. It is definitely a flaw and is contradictive to the original beliefs and intentions where God could or would spread sincerity, love and spiritual benevolence. Now the wishes are the same, but we don't always get what we wish for; especially when efforts and praying only goes so far and luck isn't very dependable.

How dependable is the belief of God? God is a word, not a thing or a person or even an anything. Once again, how can anyone believe in a word?

A word is "only" a word. It isn't enough to put one's whole heart and soul into. Sure, that whole heart and soul can be put into our own individual spirit because we are real! Depending on a person or thing that doesn't present any substance, appearance or even a word for identification as mentioned before, isn't dependable at all. That's what conventional religion is about; believing one hundred percent without doubt or even asking any exposing questions of which they have no make sense answers to anyway. Man named the word God; not a God.

The word God can be considered a spiritual deception or misunderstanding of spiritual phenomena. Flaws are noticed as we proceed. If there was a God so unbelievably powerful as man is trained to believe and is an image and likeness of us or reversed, wouldn't we be close relatives to that entity? Relatives talk to one another and of course, a lot more. This is only one indication the belief of

God as an alive entity is pure fallacy in belief. More flaws exist in that belief.

The word God can also be utilized as a representative of spirituality personally operated by the self within. The "spirit" of God is that which we experience within our own selves, not anything outside ourselves. There are no flaws in that concept.

We live on this planet on our own merits with our inner spiritual qualities, guidance and strengths. That's natural.

Now we must be able to recognize the flaws in conventional religion to pull us "all" out of this magnetism and place our consciousness into a spiritual state of reality. We must escape the grossly misunderstood clutching of conventional spirituality. We must adopt the spiritual consciousness of fully accepting responsibility for our existence, welfare and self-assurance. There is no need for worshipping something or "somebody" who isn't realistically there or anywhere else.

When we allow ourselves to become dependent on "a" God, which is nonexistent, we have surrendered our own birthright power to strongly believe in our own sustaining selves. "That" self-sustaining power was meant to be if anything was.

Animals have that strength. After they are born, reared and on their own, there are no weak and dependent animals or insects etc. Only mankind invented an ongoing dependency state of mind which prompted a needed belief in a Supreme Being.

Religious and spiritual transformation is reducing mental and emotional dependence on an unknown and incommunicable image as what we have mistakenly fantasized and referred to as a Supreme Being, God, a God or god, many Gods or gods, son of God (no daughters), God's helpers and representatives.

Now we are releasing that facade of old time and deceiving concept of power confusingly called

God and relieving ourselves of invalid and outdated beliefs in an inevitable and overdue religion to strictly spiritual consciousness within of the self and future. This is humanly developing.

Chapter 7

Does a divine entity have to "qualify?"

Is God a he, a she, an it or something? Is God a man, a woman or an animal? How about a cloud or something else? It's awkward to talk about God without saying "He" as though God was the gender of a man.

God, as unbelievably big as he must be to handle the limitless space of the universe, certainly must be something we can identify with other than Jesus who was just a man programmed from birth to play a specific religious role in crusading for his ideas of redemption and soul saving etc.

Where did God come from? When was he born? Where was he born? Was he born at all? No one knows anything about "Him" as big and powerful as people seem to believe he is. He must have a super palace somewhere in space, certainly not on planet Earth.

Well, if he's not on Earth, how would he get here quick enough in an emergency from billions of miles out in space? Oh yes, that's right, he could just "beam up" or "beam down" in seconds from wherever he was. Sounds unreal? It isn't any more unreal than the unreal views of conventional religion's supernatural or miraculous feats of which are both about the same.

People have been talking about God since they invented him thousands of years ago and still don't know "anything" about him other than what they have conjured about him.

How unfortunately unaware we were being born as images and likenesses of him when we have no idea what he looks like or whether he even has looks at all.

He must not have had any sentiment for us at all to leave us so unprepared and "on our own" on this world without "any" knowledge from "Him" or his whereabouts! That doesn't sound like a leader of any kind and doesn't sound like one of our choice.

How did we ever elect him to be our permanent leader? He didn't even tell us he wanted the job. Leaders "show" themselves. The only phenomenal "act of God" we have ever heard of or experienced were earthquakes, hurricanes, tornados, tsunamis, major floods, volcanic eruptions and that's all bad . . . for us. Wind, rain and sun seem to be a little more basically acceptable, but not particularly viewed as Godly driven even by divine belief unless that belief dictates God controls "everything" and mankind has no choices in their destiny. That's another story. Those acts of God may not have been by "any" God.

What is God qualified to do as if this long believed leader really existed? There are no "real" make sense stories of what this believed entity really did; only author devised stories by men. The only thing said about what God said in the Bible was about what "men" said God said, not actually what any God said.

Believing in something or someone is great if we can fully understand how qualified that thing or person is. So many of us have unquestionably "believed in God" because someone said to or read about. Once again, it isn't "nearly" enough to believe in.

Expecting miracles from an unidentifiable and uncommunicating entity is an unreasonable and irrational request or aspiration. Much more dependable results of desire can be accomplished and as repeatedly said, unfold when one learns how to and practices believing in the self as the power source of anything reasonably or realistically acquirable. Wishing or expecting something for no effort at all can be very disappointing. That is why "belief," in the archaic sense of believing in God functions so incoherently as in its cycling state of transforming to more qualified concepts of responsible spirit within. It does not adapt to inconceivable and unidentifiable places as unrealistically stated from religious views.

The only one qualifying to be a leader in anything is the one or God who has had subordinate experience in any field of endeavor with acquired skills for that activity. What ability does a "nonexisting" entity have for leading a changing universe, Earth and all its living beings or whatever else?

A qualification of any leader is to communicate with the followers. So far, that has only happened in unproven stories of ancient religion; certainly not enough to base an obviously needed belief system on.

Let's assume there has been a human thinking kind of God around forever. That's a mind conceiving test in itself let alone basis for evaluating spiritual transformation. Forever, back then, undoubtedly wasn't the beginning of everything, but it's enough for this scenario. That entity certainly would think much further, deeper and smarter, to say the least, than any of us. Why would that humongous entity, while creating and maintaining or even just watching everything in the space of all universes be interested in doing anything with "requests," if you will, from humans? Conventionally religious people appear to believe he will in spite of all rationale supporting the probability he won't.

Actually, qualified or not, the transformation "is" in process and won't "require" authorization, qualification or any other preliminary stamps of approval for beliefs to change. They just change! It's real helpful, though, for the people involved to address possibilities and probabilities for allowing changes to occur in a nonresistant realizing and overall blending manner for the benefit of everyone. We want to keep our sense of trust.

No one "really" knows anything about an alive existence of "God" or not. However, it's refreshing for everyone to know we can "choose" philosophies or guidelines of some nature for nurturing beliefs within our own selves as the transformation moves along with the passage of time. It "is" another growth process and growth requires promoting with effort extended.

Everyone can devise their own methods of change within themselves. When progress in anything moves along readily, help will always be available. Self-spirituality "is" moving along for each one of us as we choose.

Some may view transformation of beliefs as different, strange or even a little mystic similar to the way conventional religion began way back, but it "is" unfolding in peaceful and mature coherence because interpretation doesn't and won't vary anywhere near religious manners of the past.

Being dependent on an unqualified leader of which no one knows anything about will eventually be ancient history. People are decreasing their dependent needs of being constantly educated and reminded how or which way to spiritually believe by so many conventionally authorized leaders who lack broad and uninhibited perspective for reviewing and contributing toward much overdue spiritual change.

The only ones who will really contribute to these changes, at least for now, are the ones who have already adapted to practicing these changes plus the ones who will as a result of reading these and other texts of this nature; hence the occurring momentum of ongoing transformation. The people are and will be the qualifiers of their self-directed destiny.

More insight on one's destiny is elaborated in your author's book entitled "Paradoxes Of Destiny Explained" which covers a wide range of viewpoints, beliefs and perceptions. It tends to unravel and clarify how one word can represent what happens with everyone and everything in every way. It is a study of available options that may influence insight for growth, change or even justify present mannerisms of belief pertaining to what may control the individual, planet Earth and/or the whole universe and is not zeolous, fanatic or begoted; only assertively revealing.

If the conventional belief of God is conclusively proven or proven by God himself, if you will, concerns of self-perpetuated destiny may relax possibly because that may truly mean God is running everything. That would mean we are only the puppets who are led around. If that is the case, any of our concerns about "anything" will be deemed invalid. Saying that even sounds ridiculously illusionary and unrealistic because of this contention.

Everything stated in this book is supportive to and with mankind's qualified spiritual abilities independent of conventional beliefs and practices. Let us "all" see what is real and what may not be.

Chapter 8

The usual and unusual coming into view

Learning anything is exposing oneself voluntarily, by someone else or by influence from cultural or educational requirements; rarely from unadulterated or uninfluenced desire.

Upon just learning to walk, which is instinctual and not necessarily taught, the Asian people taught their young how to bow and they continued that form of respect to others the rest of their lives. Actually, they didn't learn how primarily out of respect, they learned how because someone "taught" them how before they could make choices. This is a form of cultural exploitation similar to attending church service. That was typical or "usual" for those people.

Most Asian nations, India and others practiced Buddha rituals and meditation etc. as a way of life which was not to be disputed. That was ancient culture and not particularly considered to be religious worshipping. That was also the usual way of learning about life which was and still is a belief of suspending or surrendering personal desires for inner peace and stability. They learned quickly in life to adhere to that manner of believing. That was and still is a system of very disciplined spirituality with much less spiritual confusion and questioning as compared to the majority of conventional beliefs of God.

Christians, Muslims and Jews may deem Buddhism as unusual because of their not believing in a mystical or supernatural being called God, Allah or whatever else in the same way.

Atheists and agnostics either didn't learn enough about the spiritual aspect of the word God to extrapolate what could be learned about spirit within the self or they learned "too" much from analyzing religious and disciplinary views pertaining to common man-made beliefs perpetuated through the process of conventional indoctrination. That's what has been happening.

One cannot learn too much in academic studies. That builds a base for dealing with social reality. However, learning too much in conventional religion leads one to be firmly and inflexibly set or creates many questions concerning conventional religion that can only be explained in terms of misled stories, not substantiated reality because of believing without evidence.

Learning about anything spiritual through money oriented leaders in the spiritual business can easily chase spiritual learning people into atheism or agnosticism when they finally detect the supporting fallacies of outdated beliefs conventional religion professes.

Conventional religion teaches and supports only what has been established by men, not any such God as they claim. They have withheld answering questions that may expose or discredit conventional beliefs concerning God or any other adjacent figures of supreme nobility. They won't answer those questions with any make sense rationale because, without saying, they very quietly agree with the agnostic view where they just don't know! Explaining it in established religious terms doesn't fully or realistically answer the questions people really need to know. That's usual with the religious leaders, but controversially unusual for the masses who desire to know what is commonly referred to as "the truth."

Where there are unknowns and secrets being held back and covertly disregarded for vast periods of time, we have better reason to be suspicious and interrogate further for absolute truth even though it does not exist in a world of reality where truth is more than just believing.

Maintaining the usual beliefs do not allow room in the consciousness of mankind for expanding into realms of reality for surviving in a world of unusual changes. If it wasn't for "having" to make these changes, because they are there and moving along with forward momentum, the status quo may have remained usual.

Now, though, archaic beliefs are fading and new concepts of spiritual accomplishments are rising on the horizon of their inevitable growth.

Spirituality of being more efficiently responsible for our existence and destiny "is" on the move and is excitingly unusual while blending away from outdated belief practices to self-sustaining security.

Traveling through new skies or caves are always unusual, but the fruit of those ventures are also rewarding.

Sure, everything coming in new is a little unusual. Finding a new mate, winning a war, graduating from college, moving to a new city, getting a better job, even winning the lottery are all a little unusual, but look at the rewards from just those few mentioned.

This short chapter is dedicated to encouraging everyone, including the very set in their ways to see only opportunity in releasing the old and ringing in the new without fear. There are no secrets around here. Everyone has and will have access to very open spirituality within the self of which will allow everyone to live with and experience the comfort and security of having their own spiritual entity within which can have any name one chooses; even God. The new spirituality is flexible.

That last statement of choice is made to indicate the use and spirit of practicing and believing in a form of spirituality with the term or feeling of "God" must never be denied by anyone as long as one believes that term and belief is "within" the self and not a belief of a someone or something of which one may believe is, if you will, "lurking" around in space or wherever one may fantasize to pull a power act of some sacrilegious nature seemingly good or whatever else. We must all be reasonably prudent, discretionary, patient, flexible and humble in our efforts of adapting to another spiritual approach in believing. Check them out thoroughly.

Chapter 9

How spiritually knowledgeable are we?

Prehistoric man, which according to science research, evolved in different stages hundreds of thousands of years ago which was an ancient time span prior to the nonestimated time of the Bible's Adam and Eve arrival. Early man had all he could do for surviving with brain power needed in being careful not to get eaten by the great animals. Food and water was plentiful. Boredom was probably unknown. It was, obviously, an animal type life of humanoids in that ancient era of time.

The period of time between early humanoids and the beginning stages of spiritual consciousness was unmeasurably vast. Humans had learned to walk and run etc., etc., but had no need to intellectually figure and analyze what spirit or God was or wasn't. That must have been real pleasant not having to worry (figuring/analyzing) about following man's established rules of preparing for an ascension into another place with their mind for a time of which they couldn't even comprehend.

Updating us to now, how could we (whatever we might be after death) even with the broadest stretch of our minds comprehend ascending to a flaming place called hell forever and ever? Only a very sadistically inclined human could have arrived at that manner of punishment; certainly not a "good" God. Heaven and hell ideas were conjured up by ancient religious innovators and doesn't presently fit in with spiritual views and beliefs of the now and future.

The terms and/or beliefs of God verses the devil are compared here to gold and silver. Gold is always more valuable and popular than silver. God will always be more valuable and popular than the devil. Besides, if there was or is a God, that God who would control all time and everything in it certainly wouldn't allow a devil in it! From that logical deduction, the concept and belief of an actual devil is nonexistent. If a devil can be deemed nonexistent through logic, a God can too. Why?

There will always be good and bad. One will not exist without the other unless we use our intellectual sense of logic in eliminating them both. We can think, say and believe there is no good or bad and it becomes true. We replace the two with just what "is" and no more; which is to say what is—is regardless of our interpretation of what we think it is.

Once we understand more rationally how to deal with good and bad, we occupy our minds with what "works" the best within our own minds, not with what someone says to do or "else."

How we believe occurs #1 as a result of how much and what kind of knowledge we presently have, #2 how we choose to be exposed as time passes and/or #3 how we purposely program our minds with our chosen exposure. That's what the self does to and with the self whether it is chosen by the self or directed by someone else.

Programming data can be derived from spiritual or nonspiritual influence. Reading, watching or listening are programming influence which forms us the way we are and will be. We must be careful with what we want to think, be and believe or we can surely become victims of others who have become very professional at feeding doctored up data into our psyches for purposes of hooking us into their methods of thinking, believing and being. Many people love practicing those methods of manipulating people's minds; especially in conventional religion.

Being spiritual minded, as mentioned, is great or maybe just helpful at times. There's nothing required by anyone or entity to be spiritual on a constant bases and spirituality has no connections with any man-made contentions of spiritual sources outside our bodies. It's all within. Anything to the contrary is unreal and only perceived as wishing in fantasy.

The commandments written on stone plates was a very clever and time consuming plan, as was so many other so called miracles, devised by Moses and clan to control his insecure and desperate people. According to the Bible's story, Moses became angry with his people for unjustifiably partying while he went into the mountains to get the plates from "God" of which he broke into pieces. He returned to the mountains and brought back more of them from "God." He probably carved them himself since he was in the mountains for days.

The stone plates were eventually crowned and placed into an elaborately sealed container referred to as the Arch of the Covenant. Originally, these commandments were believed to be sent by God and weren't really covenants. Covenants are agreements made by more than one person. The commandments on stone were just that; commands supposed by God to abide by or pay the consequences for being so evil. It was just a manipulation to calm his people down for organizing them.

One must remember; all the written claims of what God ever supposedly said or did were preliminarily planned and subjugated the masses of people into further challenges of survival. Multiple centuries have passed and so very many people still believe those man-made stories. Many "others" are noticing the flaws in them and are blending in with transforming spirituality of our unfolding eras of time.

The sealed covenants haven't and may not be shown because modern inspection will reveal the fact mankind made them, not any God. That would lead to the final contest where inevitable conventionally religious believing could very easily sway off to the wayside and conform to oncoming spiritual transformation.

Beside the story of the stone plates, why didn't anyone ever pick up the broken pieces of the plates Moses broke? For the sake of historic records, personal collection or many other reasons, one would think those pieces would fit into the records.

Learning a subject only adds to knowledge of that subject. That's limited knowledge. Learning as much as possible of opposite views on the subject adds a much larger perspective for evaluating how well the subject or its details fit in with one's life. That's the value of what may seem grossly irritating "or" revivingly refreshing depending on how open, set or flexible one may be in their scope of learning beyond what they already know or believe.

Everyone wants to know the truth so they can know which avenue to travel on the road of belief. Someone can easily say, "This is the truth" or "Believe this way and you will know the truth."

Moving in a direction someone said to go and you will find the truth may be moving into a mistaken direction to find a desired satisfaction of what so many indoctrinated people inappropriately refer to as absolute truth. That's only a claim from representatives of conventional religion to support their conglomerated beliefs, contentions and indoctrinating methods.

Truth is not what someone says it is. Truth is what an individual acquires from observing and realistically analyzing as many angles as possible for forming a belief of it. Spiritual knowledge is individually acquired practical, useful and logical information supported with calm feelings, not habitual tendencies. A little more on truth is presented in the next chapter.

Religious transformation "is" a little unusual after all those years of the same habits. It is to spiritually search for and identify that stronger, friendlier more acceptably established "self-image" for programming whatever is desired within the self by spiritual choices or even if one chooses the terminology;

God within. It's like talking to the conventional aspect of God, except now it becomes that "power" of God transformed from the usually believed God outside the self to the same power within. That power within is no longer referred to as "God." We don't need "names" for our power, beliefs, security and confidence in ourselves unless one "chooses" to name it.

After all, the term God represents belief power in any language and becomes human power over mind and body when internally developed through belief within. That power "is" real, not a fictitious supplement of conventional belief. Again, that power is used effectively within and has no connection with any mystical or so called supernatural being. One "must" utilize patience in self-spiritual power at least until it is confidently developed. The result will be wonderfully obvious.

Nonbelievers now have something they can work with in their own privacy like when one meditates, programs or prays within, not to something externally which has never securely been understood.

These transforming beliefs of the power of God within have been arising from a misconception of their being a Supreme Being out in space somewhere; somehow. That's part of the very slow transformation of believing which we are probing into.

Unusual as it may seem to many, others are discovering it is becoming a way of life not because your author proclaims it to be, but because this spiritual transformation is obviously overdue in ascending throughout human consciousness similarly to how conventional religion was in the ancient and more recent past.

A God out in space doesn't show signs of being real. Power of God and self-belief is the same here inside all of us to be used for survival purposes. Recognizing it is growing into it.

That's what this fuss in spirituality is all about. Spirit of God is spirit of belief within, not fictitious, supernatural and unprovable.

Latch on to the power of spirituality within and be free to gain confidence of it and much more.

Chapter 10

Mankind's birth of God

Religion wasn't always "just there." It began when mankind had enough sense in his brain to realize they were feeling insecure which we now understand was a form of loneliness and psychological hunger in longing for something to feel secure with other than their bare essentials and family. They couldn't understand it or know how to express it in the few communicable words they knew at that time, so it evolved slowly.

There wasn't many people in those ancient times. Family and clans were thinly spaced. That was a time when humanoids were animalistic, but did suffer from emotional insecurity. Fighting amongst their indigenous neighbors caused more insecurities and increased their hunger for reducing their anxieties to be aggressive to other aggressors.

Their insecurity was tied to a lack of direction as to where they were going in life. Before the times of advancing progress, there wasn't much to do beside eat, sleep, chant and have children etc.

Their instinctual urges and drive attracted them onward toward "more" fulfillment than just their basic needs. Their yearning desire to form a believing function along with basic needs slowly led them in a direction of acquiring mental consciousness.

They were still evolving from their animalistic mannerisms to a state of developing language, making clothes and logically organizing their lives as the centuries and millenniums passed.

Next in their mental growth of consciousness came a mental spirit. Thoughts of believing were born and wavered unsteadily like a change of weather. Those thoughts of believing formed and reformed along with their increasing ability to rationally and verbally communicate. This was also part of their evolutionary growth in time.

Eventually, through their stages of mental growth, they developed basic standards of believing that allowed them ability to accelerate in communicating for purposes of human progress which led to chanting wishes or beliefs, celebrating social accomplishments and artistically drawing with their newly acquired imagination in their crude and unpolished mannerisms of that ancient era of time.

Over the centuries and millenniums, they became erect standing, objective minded and had even a stronger desire for security. The more they progressed in their evolutionary momentum, the more they wanted to know. It became an obsession and they needed something more than their speedily acquired knowledge.

They were pursuing their way through life suffering growing pains while their social coherence was dissipating with no solutions in sight for returning to the peace and serenity of the simpler past. Sound familiar even in this age of time?

Eventually, with more development over long periods of time, everything they thought, said, chanted for or sang became actual or real in many ways. They discovered "reality" and became more aware of their consciousness to rationalize, choose, fantasize or dream. Mankind was fine with reality. It taught them to survive better after they acquired that intellectual ability. They were outgrowing their animalistic inherence and evolving into mind maturing humans as compared to the mental limits of their animal predecessors.

Why all this evolutionary history? There are two states of spiritual mind. One is living, believing and practicing within bounds of reality. The other is living, believing and practicing within bounds of nonreality. One of which they tell us is true and one of which they tell us in not true. It's up to each one of us to determine what "is" real and what "isn't" real. More study on "both" sides gets it! Patience pays.

Evolutionary history of man, how their beliefs originated and developed into the majority of present day spirituality is one view worth delving into.

Another view states Earth wasn't even here and suddenly God made it along with all the universe. Then he placed Adam and Eve on it somewhere in a mysterious time before the time of Abraham, Moses and Jesus etc. This is also worth delving into for comparison purposes. Some will get it quick. Others will ponder.

The just of these comparisons is for each person to individually weed out what makes sense from what does not make sense. Just because something is stated in a book by supposed witnesses going on thousands of years ago doesn't make it true; not at all! This is the time to conserve on their opinionated beliefs, hearsay and ingeniously contrived literature.

What makes anything spiritually true or not is the realization of what logically "can" happen with human beings by analyzing the unfolding of mankind's progress as far back as history concretely records it and estimates further back based on research from those records plus present geological, geophysical, religious and other interrogational surveys. This examination is held as enough or not enough evidence to believe its truth until the other side of spiritual contention is examined as follows:

Evidence is, again, needed to substantiate what is generally believed in conventional religion. If one only listens, reads and believes based on customary, culturally or family tradition, that's power for the religious institutions to reign and there probably won't be another side allowed to view with any patience. However, if people let their programmed beliefs relax for awhile, they may acquire enough insight to evaluate many questions usually not answered by church officials other than "just believe" for determining which religion, spiritual philosophy and/or other beliefs can truthfully be accepted. Acceptance is a pretty good basis for believing anything religious, scientific "or" what we may term as "actual," but let's accept what is "real."

Back to early mankind, the more they utilized their maturing mind ability, which was a partner to their spirituality within, the more satisfactorily communicable they became with language. That, in turn, allowed them to search more for their lingering desire to become more secure within other than the basics mentioned. The people felt very insecure and needed something to fulfill that need.

One day, a man said he heard a voice. The voice said, "Come outside." The man went outside and the voice said, "I am the source of security you and your people have been longing for. I am here and you can depend on me to help you through life. Just believe in me." The man was so excited, he spread the word of this mystic entity and they believed him. They were all looking too. The belief in what that entity supposedly said was so strong, they gave that believed entity a name which was changed several times and finally to "God." The people rejoiced. Those details may not be precisely accurate, but that's how the belief in God started in the pre-Hebrew days and perpetuated through to Abraham, Moses, Mary and others so it goes in the Bible.

We know the approximate dates of the above people. Scientists now have calculated eras of early man going back as far as two million years to the time of homeo habolis before the time of homeo sapiens.

The likelihood of mankind dating back to evolutionary times hold's more credibility than the religious view because the Bible states God made the universe and Adam and Eve much closer to the time of modern man (let's say four to five thousand years or so) which excludes multiple million years or more of earth, plant and animal to man growth.

The conflicting dates of time cancels out any validity of a Supreme Being; especially a "He." Science has already proven Earth, Moon and Mars are multimillions of years old if not more. Religious contentions based on the Bible are "way" off course from historical and logical deduction. What is left? Spiritual power within and it is growing stronger than ever.

The following is another view of how the Bible invalidates its contentions, history and truths: The Bible's contention of God making the heavens, Earth and all in and on it is defeated because the Bible text indicated it all happened sometime in the general era of time as described in the Bible's beginning. According to that, suddenly Adam and Eve popped up as the first people somewhere around four thousand years ago as though there wasn't an evolutionary period of time at all.

Shortly after, according to the way it was written, Abraham appeared, then Moses etc. somewhere between a very broad guess of two to three thousand years ago since dates aren't available.

Mankind's scientific and geological research concerning their timely growth descends into hundreds of thousands of years to identifiable human evidence proving they evolved from "their" lower state relatives etc. in the beginning of all human type beings.

Mankind wasn't instantly formed like we appear today. Accepted specimens have proven mankind passed through many long periods of time in their slow growth of time. Beside all that, astronomers have discovered the heavens of the universe are older than they can calculate. That means whoever wrote God's beginning didn't have a clue of what they were talking about except they probably knew the public would believe it anyway and they did.

Even the story of Noah and his arc doesn't add up. There would be no way of rounding up all those animals from around the world that quick when the supposed sudden downpour of rain occurred; especially with uncontrolled, wild and man-eating animals. In those days, they didn't have large containers of water to bring onto the boat. The food would have rotted away and mass panic would have set in plus the overloaded boat would have seeped water in and sunk in the horrendous storms of water. They didn't have the technology or equipment to build boats that large as we do now. It's all a story of fictional fantasy just like movie making.

People will do or believe "anything" to make fantasy seem real for their pleasure or security. Think about it and gain more confidential security. Ignore it and possibly be swept into it as a great many followers of history did.

Chapter 11

Why so many religions?

Any organized religious belief is considered conventional in these texts. They all place their spiritual beliefs in a Supreme Being. History tells of various gods which were idolized with the use of carved statues. Some of those statues represented religious sector beliefs and some were for authoritative and hierarchical control over subserviently natured and "kept" people.

Spiritual transformation of godly beliefs occurred in these precalender days too. The people found less practical use for material objects as statues and also discovered God was never seen and was only felt in the minds of the people. They developed a belief of a soul and that traveled fast around the countryside. There was no stopping them. The transformation from animalistic existence to something spiritual was new and a bit awkward in its adaptation, but it couldn't be stopped. That's the way transformations are. It grew for centuries.

Religious formations of churches and crusaders spread the word of God around the countryside's preaching their newly acquired faith. It gained momentum across the land similar to a gold rush.

There was nothing to sell then except religious statements and spiritual security. Church growth and its competition expanded phenomenally. Ministers, Rabbis, pastors and other clergymen became as popular as entertainers and their income began growing too when established barter began for religious service.

Over time, another church popped up and their rules, beliefs and religious dogma changed for their particular advertising benefits. Centuries of church crusading and expansion of "all" the central themed churches spread further throughout the Middle East and elsewhere. They achieved spiritual dominance which has been indirectly attempting government intervention for more political control. There are now lingering signs of a quiet battle for religious supremacy on the horizon. Rules of peace, religious love and cooperation of the past are beginning to exhibit their magnetism of hierarchy domination. This new spiritual transformation "can" offset that possibility. Now, though, it will happen through the people, not organizations.

Even though so very many people want conventional religious change to create and maintain peace and serenity, the religious organizations have been slowly gathering worldwide power to influence or direct a form of religious power as a government which could require everyone to conform to their outdated mannerisms of belief. The transformation can alter that situation.

Why so many religions now? The amount now could be the beginning of a super religious wave of conventional religious indoctrinators or better still; monopolizers. Once it gains momentum against this oncoming spiritual transformation, it may be difficult to reverse because of the power conventional religion has had for so long. That is a possible reality. However, this is only a speculation at this time.

Breaking down through faults and contradictions as it has been doing, the common religious institutions are now like a huge cloud ready to rain their outdated religious dogma onto innocent, naive and vulnerable people to keep the "system" going and initiate the so called truth into their heads.

People are now asking when did God begin. The conventional answers do not satisfy smarter people now as compared to those older time days of inflexible religious training.

The evolution of man and religion has uncovered many unforeseen surprises as one would never have suspected in the unbelievable growth which conventional religion has passed through. So many churches have been built, rebuilt or permanently demolished from fires, wars, floods, earthquakes and mortgage foreclosures.

Many times when those unfortunate incidents happen, the religious organizers expand with more churches and the memberships expand too. That has been the religious progress of the past.

Churches are about the only way we experience religion beside praying anywhere. Different denominations sprung up everywhere as the gold rush of religion progressed many centuries or more ago and up to recently. New ideas and changes to support the main theme of believing in God brought in new ambitious clergymen with new righteousness principles thereby accrediting conventional religion with more power than ever to emotionally dominate people.

Each new denomination had significantly different reasons for claiming new religious philosophy. That has been a historical evolution too; some spiritually different, some organizationally different, some more conservatively strict and some just the opposite.

There has been, as we know, religious type organizations with barbarous rules of chopping off limbs and/or sacrificing lives for either ritualistic beliefs or penalties paid from disobedience. That sets a bad example for any spiritually oriented belief system; definitely a flaw in religious belief.

So many or maybe even too many religions are usually quantitatively parallel with the demographic sections of the country, state, city or county. Where there are many people, there are usually many churches. Where there are various denominations, there can be churches of various beliefs. Where there are ethnic variations in the country, there probably won't be enough churches for them. If they live in large cities, they usually have plenty of access to religions for them to choose.

Having many religions is like having many different beliefs. That's the privilege of living in a country where one can exercise freedom to believe.

The issue is not primarily whether a belief is right or not. It's whether a person has evaluated and freely chosen a route of belief that "appears" right, knows he or she can get all the necessary amenities and tolerate any disappointments pertaining to that manner of believing.

There are great advantages of having so many religions. Visiting and/or studying as many as possible gives one wider scope perspective in comparing them and further perspective when comparing that first perspective to the spiritual believing within. Going to one church with one type of belief isn't even a start for evaluating what is right for the self. There are great advantages in checking out many churches and beliefs to really know what may help in the process of understanding which road may be chosen for spiritual or maybe even nonspiritual fulfillment. The individually chosen road is the "right" road for the self. Enough selves will tell more about the "truth."

Whenever "anyone" says, "God says so," "It's what God wants", "It was God's plan to have all those churches" or anything else supposedly said by God, it's what human's choose to think and believe what God said. They have no knowledge of what any spiritual entity may be thinking or if there is any of that type of "thinking" at all. There are no assurances or guarantees of "anything" pertaining to what we have been "taught" about God or even what has been superficially transformed from early mankind's hunger for something bigger than themselves. That bigger entity, which has been extensively argued over was "invented" by man, not even women.

Now, if "God" was in control of everything like when man says it's God's will or God's plan, we'll wait for God to handle it or whatever else, then once again, we would have nothing to do, think or say about anything anytime waiting for God. That includes, for instance, saying or even thinking about what God says, thinks or does. We would be like puppets on a string without consciousness, opinion, drive or anything similar.

The seemingly rational assumption where "we," not any God, have had all control over ourselves suggests humans were the only ones who invented, initiated the ideas of and built all places of worship throughout the world ourselves without any type of help from a supposed Supreme Being.

When we believe "we" are at the helm of our destiny to create mountains and promote our lives and everything in them, we can "run" our spiritual minds and lives better than ever free of so many of those said inhibiting, restricting and uptight conventional beliefs of the ancient past.

Those of us who are practicing this spiritually self-reliant responsibility are becoming better people for everyone and will continue with this spiritual philosophy and belief while others blending into it will be doing the same.

Their are so many religions on this earth; not just because of so many different views of how to accept God particularly, how to compete and show more righteousness for monopolizing the business of spirituality etc., etc., but because mankind hasn't been able to thoroughly focus in and agree on this perception of what God is except for what the original religious innovators, preachers, authors, lexicographers, exploiters and proverbial know-it-alls have professed.

If mankind's "God" was so caring and wanted to be coherently worshipped as he really "is," he would let mankind know very easily if he is so supernatural instead of directing mankind to carry on so awkwardly, gullibly and unknowledgeably uninformed about what God really is or maybe really isn't. Read the list in back about "What God Is And Is Not."

Chapter 12

Basis for believing or not

Some people believe anything they hear because they are so incredibly open "or" just plain gullible or naive. That can be a very confusing state of mind believing everything which usually ends in "mixed feelings" where having ready access to both sides "just in case" one doesn't work, the other may. It becomes guesswork causing more insecurity in believing. Many times, one may give up with an indifferent attitude that goes nowhere while continuing with an unsatisfactory "habit" of believing.

Other people resist almost everything suggested or promoted by anyone with their ultra conservative, set and righteous attitudes and wouldn't even support a belief that might save someone's life.

Is the interim attitude any better? That might be for maintaining social friendship and compatibility if that's the main objective at the time. Again, that's like standing on the fence with no real belief. It doesn't do much for supporting the spiritual character inside the self that represents what or how the self really believes or thinks.

Placing oneself in a position where one can fully as possible learn and understand the pros and cons of "both" sides is a much better position to be in for determining what individual truth may amount to. That requires what may seem like endless patience and that is a significant factor in determining the "way to go" in the world of spiritual belief.

The belief, desire or strong contentions of absolute truth has been searched for and contended to be as long as mankind has thought of it without any agreed resolution. One can qualify for understanding what an absolute truth is if one has a rationally accepted ability to comprehend and describe where the end of space is plus describe how "God" can exist as being technically "real" without using the power of belief in that contention. Otherwise, there is no absolute truth; only wishful thinking and/or belief which is usually applied to those who have been religiously indoctrinated in one way or another.

Believing only, without substantiation other than just that, is just not enough for all to agree about concerning an absolute existence especially of a completely "unknown" figure conventionally referred to as a Supreme Being.

Believing in one's self, generally, can be just as disputatious as its independence of outside the self-influence. Everyone has a birthright privilege to choose a manner of spiritual belief. No one has to wait for any supposed master to decide what one's destiny may amount to. That's ours to decide. If we don't want to know, then we may become circumstantial victims of someone or something else. Subscribing to "any" manner of belief is our debatable birthright.

Belief can originate #1 from a nonsubstance divine entity, #2 a person or group which is substance, #3 from that which can be substance, nonsubstance or both arising from family and cultural influence "or" #4 from what may be "more" fitting when one prefers to "choose" a definite route of spiritual belief after rationally searching and analyzing options.

Freedom to choose is always the best as compared to being a protoplasmic victim or subject who has to live up to planned expectations of someone else or even something that may not exist—at all. Humans have an uncanny way of devising what they want people to believe. Belief in religion is like going along with an idea without substantiation of its existence and is usually or conventionally propagated by structured organizational dogma based on imaginary desire of which attracts fantasy and fear for purposes of remaining adapted to the established and societal structure.

Spiritual believing is either believing in something, someone or the self. One must make that choice and it must be with every source possible. This isn't a choice of what church to attend or any church at all. This is a choice of remaining with conventional belief of God or transforming with and into accepting the power and security of spirituality within the self. Once that power of belief in the self is adopted, faith in the self is supported and one experiences more confidence in the self than ever. This is also a plus for nonbelievers to observe or pursue if or when they choose to.

Is there a basis for not believing too? Yes. There are four ways to be a nonbeliever; at least in a divine spiritual manner. #1 is to be born into a family of nonreligious believers who may be of nomad type tribes, #2 is for people who are deeply into metaphysical philosophy, #3 is for people who are either born into Buddhistic practices or have applied to their practices or #4 who are usually younger than older people who haven't had personal guidance in religious exposure and who "have" had exposure to more nonreligious than religious believing people.

Most of us humans are subjects of what we have been exposed to from influence of others. Resistance to those influences are gained when #1 the influence is weak or inconsistent, #2 the influence appears mixed or contradictive or #3 when one periodically or consistently moves away from those influential people.

Humans are all born with natural senses to breath, cry, laugh, eat, kick and excrete, but none of us were or are born with an innate sense to believe in religious propagation or its practices.

All living beings were and are supplied with everything we were meant to have for living purposes. Anything else has been sometimes cleverly and sometimes not so cleverly made-up by humans some of which include conventional religion.

Babies and small children can easily adapt to inborn and natural tendencies to adapt. If there really "was" a God who one could believe in, that could be considered a God given gift.

Those small children have no idea of what religion means let alone God. Even many many years later, one doesn't know what God is. How would a small child know? An adult can believe, but a young kid still won't know how to believe in anything supposedly meaningful other than what he or she is steadily taught. No children possess any God given instinct to voluntarily adapt to or study religion. If they did, they still wouldn't be able to predicate or describe what the meaning or belief was behind the dogma they learned. Many young to older people stay with religious basis out of fear, fantasy, social coherence "and" because they still haven't found what they were supposed to be looking for with all their superficial training. It started when they were we tots; when they didn't possess that innate ability to understand religious belief "in" God and they still don't have it. Of course, they won't tell anyone. That would make them look bad, stupid or indifferent. So they just keep playing the part. Basis for most religious believing is more inadequate than most people can or will admit.

Inner spiritual belief is as real as a person is alive and little fault can be found similarly to when and how a baby is born.

There just hasn't been enough emphasis, interest or natural instinct for raising spiritual consciousness within the self for comfortable and secure confidence. The time for its occurrence has finally caught up with us.

Chapter 13

Fallacies of structured belief

Fallacy means leading one or more to believe one thing or another is happening, did happen, can happen or will happen. Possibilities of a "few" people having misled others is more probable than masses of people misleading others since the masses have been the recipients of deception through institutionally administrative heritage for a very long time.

Religious heritage is almost like genetic inheritance. It not only becomes steady and habitual, it also becomes very reliable. Now, are those reliabilities leading people in the right direction in this time of spiritual transformation? Does that reliability help make people individually stronger for the up and coming challenges ahead or does it just make the fallacy oriented religious institutions stronger and richer? Which is more important and needed for becoming "self-reliable?"

Whenever the statement is made, "God loves you," it's not only an insubstantial conjecture and a complete fallacy in words, it is an attempt to religiously manipulate a person to believe in something debatably not possible. If God was truly real, that would be a valid statement. However, that would be considered a miracle. Miracles are classified as supernatural and supernatural is incomprehensible to mankind; hence, unreachable and unreal until such a time when it is proven differently. All the answers to questions as these from conventionally religious people are only answered in standard religious form passed down from heresay to heresay and in decaying literature that cannot possibly be utilized in our future consciousness for anything except old time beliefs, archive records and used book stores.

Every time a religious speaker preaches on TV, there is an overabundance of religious jargon about what God says. Man never knew anything about such an entity who supposedly rules the universe, so how could they know what that entity was thinking or saying? Even that question sounds ridiculously elementary. A belief in God as a symbol of confidence in our inner spirit to believe in ourselves is fitting, natural and "can" make sense to anyone. Nowadays, we require factually researched studies for teaching educational subjects. How on earth can we believe in a subject such as religion from archaic literature written and rewritten by several authors of their unprovable and dark age type stories? Just because it's "in the book" is no way to accept it as the truth; not at all.

Supporting a mystical figure in disguise of being nothing or whatever has no basis for making any sense. Supporting a figure seemingly "everywhere" where one cannot even point to it is also nonsensical. We are human. We have to make sense out of what might make sense. Anything else is nonsense.

That believable or unbelievable entity doesn't talk. If all the things all those ministers, pastors, clergy people and other institutional or religious people said God said had any truth to it over the centuries or much longer, there probably wouldn't be much doubt about a real existence of God. Since most of it all has no appearances of being truly proven so far, it is deducted mostly as fallacy with a slight benefit of possibility.

Church worship is usually done by keeping their heads up and some drop them down like they don't know where God is. One minute they raise their arms way up and the next minute they are kneeling with their heads drooping down. Sure, that all may be traditional with one denomination and strictly voluntary with another denomination. The churches honor and glorify God and expect the people to do the same, but most of the people only glorify God for the purpose of getting something back for themselves; they think. Most religious preaching describes misinformed stories of history and are fallacies in words. Odds of probability favor there's no one there; only the people. They seem to have to be convinced God is there and that keeps them coming back. That's what the religious industry wants.

A great deal of the Bible states what God thought, said or did. For an entity who never appears or "really" speaks, other than what people are programmed enough to believe out of a book, at church or in a movie, those scriptures state a lot about what God thought, said and did. Whenever the Bible indicates it's God's word or what God said, it's what the writers chose to believe God thought, said or did and they printed it.

So much in the Bible, other than stories of people living their lives and dealing with interpreting religious rules and laws, is what people did with or outside the rules and laws and how the "Lord" fits into it all realistically or not realistically. This is where our part comes into play checking it out.

Sin mentioned in the Bible was about man-made beliefs and contentions, not any demands made by any God. Obviously, there was plenty of jurisdiction and penalties dealing with sin and the court, such as they were judged by men, not God. "He" wouldn't show up. Besides, "He" might have been a "She" and the men wouldn't have tolerated that! The Bible is all about many misled stories published over a long period of time. The fallacies in words trickled in to the publishers over those long periods of time. Many manipulated additions and subtractions could have taken place toward the final editions. Yes, witnesses to that possibility are a little short-handed. The same applies to the possibilities in Bible versions of miracles too. There is a reasonable possibility there have been more religious fallacies in the ancient past moving forward than actual facts because of the eventual support of conventional religion.

Sunday school for children taught them how to climb up the ladder of purity to get into heaven where God was residing which appeared the best way to indoctrinate them for being dedicated to the cause of Supreme Being religion. They were right. The kids learned to believe all the religious jargon put out; so much in fact they wouldn't listen to anyone else. They grew with conventional religion as was planned "for" them the same as all the predecessors of the past did for their recipients of religious indoctrination. Ask why was it so necessary to constantly teach all that religious jargon.

If there was a God, that God would have surely been intelligent enough to let us know about "Him" in a much more cool calm and collected manner than all the misleading and misunderstanding confusion conventional religion has put us through over time.

Even though the religious teachers may have really believed in their cause possibly from a very wide perspective view of reasons, the ongoing effects on their students became profoundly vested to a point where they became indepthly and irreversibly engrossed in their system of feeling secure. That's good for their cause, but not for a wide scoped belief in nonfantasy reality. Those indepth students may encase themselves into their world of deceptive fantasy and never return to our world of reality. Ironically speaking, none of it has anything to do with religion or reality. It's all psychological which is a view of how the psychogenetic configuration of the brain processes and maintains its inherent and received mental data. That's what makes or allows us to accept a belief or not. Like anything else, that process "can" be redeveloped depending on strength of influence, how one may be willing to flex through disciplinary efforts or how one chooses to reprogram the psyche.

The meantime has it fallacy exposure puts up resistance to reprogramming efforts and that requires determination to escape the effectively established religious indoctrination.

Miracles are fallacies. Claims have been made about miracles being supernatural which is the same thing as magic. If God was magical, as we humans interpret magic as being, "He" if you will, wouldn't have had to make all of those famous people in the Bible do and act the way they did. If "He" was real and in control like so many billions have believed, "He" could have made everyone's destiny so very much different; like peaceable everywhere with that supernatural magic. "He" could have snuffed us out in a second with magic or probably without magic. Magic is only a human concept. So much, if not all of religious believing is magical and fantasy oriented; not real.

Everything thought of or attempted to practice in so called magic or supernatural manners is fallacy in action which may seem entertaining to some degree, but is phony, artificial and imitative. A great deal of normal praying wishes do come true not because of supernatural communication, but because of natural averages where they would have happened anyway without praying. Again, supporting the praying cause helps bring the odds of success to the prayer's side religiously, spiritually or nonreligiously.

Anything not real can be described in real terms as only believed like Santa Claus, outer space people and living forever. They depict fallacies in words and have no substantial or real value.

Adam and Eve has sounded like a true wonderland with all the amenities ever wanted. That was a story in fantasy made-up by a very alive human author and people bought it because they liked it and the author knew they would. That story of human life suddenly popped up out of nowhere (Genesis 5:1) with no mentioning of any type of evolutionary functioning. Why? In those days of Biblical stories, the people, let alone the author had no knowledge yet of religious or spiritual evolution and apparently God or was it Jehovah or Allah or who/whatever had no knowledge of that evolution yet either! It wasn't yet invented! This sounds like another debatable battle between what came first; evolution of the species, religious evolution, spiritual evolution or Adam and Eve.

Basic evolution is proven. The issue of Adam and Eve is not. Religious fallacies never seem to end.

The stories of Jesus preaching the good word of God may be true. However, there is no evidence except what is written in the Bible and that we know was written from many sources and translated by several people spread out over hundreds of years or more before final publishing. Plus, common writers make changes in stories written by the original authors for more dramatic effects. So, many of the stories of what Jesus said have a fair chance of being true; give or take a little. He talked about being meaningfully respectful, having moralistic values and how to adapt and spiritually believe in particular to and with a divine source which was admirable—then.

When Jesus was a boy, he confined himself to the religious institutions for learning the history, beliefs and customs of growing religion mainly because he didn't know anything about God other than what Mary taught him and didn't posses mystical power. This is contradictory to the Bible's stories were Jesus was indicated to be half God. If that "was" the case, he wouldn't have had to be educated in "any" way to say the very least.

If Jesus had real supposed powers of God, being the supposed son of God more than any other man, he would have had those mystical powers and other powers when he was a younger man too. Pertaining to Mary's pregnancy being God's magic, magic does not exist.

The indication here is Jesus was only a wise man, not basically any different than any other man. Jesus supposedly performed many miracles of which is said people saw. He knew what the power of suggestion was and used it in a hypnotic manner to heal people. It worked then and it works now as is well known. The possibility exists where that story of Jesus was only concocted by the authors of the Bible.

Beside an impressive lecturer, Jesus was a great performer. He had many followers and various assistants. The indication, suspicion and possibility here is his so called miracles were staged with his helpers who assisted him in the process of believing not only in him, but in his inevitable legacy with "God" which would inseminate the people of the future in "divine" spirituality. It worked. Now, it's being exposed.

Mary programmed Jesus so firmly to believe he was the son of God, he completely believed he was and performed the role of supporting the kingdom of heaven and a Supreme Being. He became obsessed with being a messiah and had to maintain that image to the end. He undoubtedly believed he was going to heaven.

This may sound a bit suspiciously erratical in its believable nature, but notice how many other untold deceptions and religious contradictions have been unveiled in recent history.

The theory of supernatural and magical phenomena isn't real. The nature of those "miracles" need a little more checking out.

Jesus wasn't popular with the governmental or primary religious regimes in the Middle Eastern countries. If God was real, "He" could have fixed that problem.

The Jewish institution scorned Jesus for building his own kingdom which soon led to the Roman

Empire getting control over him. He believed in God as he was "taught" by others. That meant he wasn't anything like God might have been. That's not hard to decipher.

The crucifixion wasn't about giving himself to his cause. It was about existing Empires suppressing, setting examples and eliminating him as competition which may have been a threat to their thrones.

Jesus decided to become a martyr for what he believed would become "his" kingdom in heaven forever while the Roman and Jewish Empires were quietly, in their own different ways, preparing the people to make moral and terminal judgments for the destiny of Jesus which, of course, meant death.

One mistake he made, among many others, was telling people to follow him as though he was God or something similar. Another major paradox in mistakes Jesus made in revealing his portraying image to so many of us over a period of time as being the son of God and not just an ordinary man as follows: If he was half God, which so many people seemed to have believed and still do, he would have been born with the genetic and inherent abilities to perform so called miracles at any age. He couldn't even simulate them until he was older and developed enough to "act out" those author described incidents so famously and deceivingly described in the Bible.

Many five and six year old children have performed wondrous acts of performance in music, math, computer work and other creative endeavors "without" any particularly spiritual or inherited superpowers.

Jesus didn't and/or couldn't perform "any" of his acts of miracles until he gained enough human confidence which was developed with normal maturity. The question here is when, where and why would the God powers of Jesus begin to reshape the world's people through Jesus as though he was the only so called Messiah or savior ever? He didn't practice those supposed Godly powers most of his life. He didn't know how.

Sure, anyone can devise answers to those questions and uncertainties to fit their beliefs and causes, but they won't be able to pinpoint when, if at all, Jesus acquired "any" ability to perform miracles and if he did have that ability, he could have very easily prevented his crucifixion especially when he became older, mature and confident enough to tell people he was God and to follow him. If it was true what he said, he could have proven it right there on the spot, but he couldn't and even if he was God endowed, why would he have to prove anything? He didn't really have "any" of the God power he claimed. He was only a human with an unknown father beside his step father Joseph who committed himself to being responsible for Mary in exchange for saving her from being stoned to death for blasphemy. So goes that part of the "story."

Why would a son of a God who made the universe have to be taught carpentry? All this probing and disproving becomes a little confusingly ridiculous, but wherever that ability to interrogate came from, we do have that right whether it is our freedom of birthright, a God given privilege or just because we choose to; it's available. Let's exercise it!

After Jesus died and was supposedly placed in the tomb with a heavy stone door placed over the entrance, the "story" has it he appeared outside the tomb with a few people, but they could have been a few who weren't known which means they couldn't really identify this man as really being Jesus. They all dressed in well covered robes with beards, mustaches and long hair. It was very easy to devise a substitute of Jesus for a short period of time and then conveniently disappear after a few dramatic and fictitious words of wisdom. Jesus was obviously taken away and buried or cremated.

His mother Mary and surrogate father Joseph wept for him knowing he was dead. The dead do not return to life. Nothing dead ever returns to life. It never has and never will. That only exists in fantasy and believing. It's only in the mind and only in the book; nowhere else.

Abe Lincoln, John Kennedy, Martin Luther King and Jesus Christ all had a vision. They were all good men with good purposes, intentions and goals. In spite of their sincere efforts, they were all murdered in cold blood. None of them "gave" their lives to death for "any" cause. They wanted to live too.

Jesus didn't "give" his life so "certain" people could go to heaven. That's only a "human" thought and belief. Jesus was crudely and sadistically murdered without him having any choice in the matter. He was only a victim of his beliefs and putty in the hands of his executioners. He was only a human being and they killed him like the others mentioned in a merciless manner.

The following is a "human" thought: God sent this man Jesus into the human system of living for purposes of converting man's sinful ways into repentance to and with "Him." Surely, God wouldn't want Jesus to be hurt or tortured for doing good deeds because God is a good God. That seems to be a common belief about God. Would "God" think that way? We don't know "anything" about what "God" is or does other than what is printed in a book. How could we possibly know anything about whether Jesus was just a guy, an assistant to God, a son of a God, no different than anyone else or even if he was specially sent to Earth at all?

"God" could have just plopped anyone in on Earth for his purpose if he was so supernaturally magical instead of allowing or directing such a cruel manner of humanistic entanglement to happen.

Remember, this is about a supposedly admired entity of billions of people over time "who," if you will, could change bad situations to good situations if he was everything as good as his inventors, promoters and supporters have envisioned or pretended him to be.

Some of the questionable stories of Jesus and Mary's Immaculate Conception are either true, an unfortunate misconception, a deliberate deception or an outright lie. There are several possibilities where Mary, a young, beautiful and undoubtedly sensuously appearing woman could have become pregnant in several different ways even though, as was stated in the famous book of many authors, she supposedly adhered to the vows of chastity.

Based on the belief and evidence where supernatural and magic phenomena do not exist, Mary was either unaware of how she became pregnant or she just didn't tell the truth. Millions, if not billions, of people have been untruthful to save themselves from scrutiny, embarrassment and/or scorn if not more serious judgments. There is still no evidence of anything supernatural or magical. Our universe is real, not supernatural, magical or the opposite of real. The opposite of real is "nothing."

This chapter has been a contributing part for religious interrogation needed in passing through the belief transformation period of time which "is" happening.

Chapter 14

Value of religious transformation

Religious or spiritual transformation, which are quite relative, are definitely not something that has been planned by revolutionists or coalitionists who want control over people's minds and money; not at all! There is no one religious, political, philosophical, scientific group or organization forming the transformation. It is forming like the clouds in the sky for rain over dry land or how peace "or" war moves along and cannot be stopped. How about how an entertainer gains fame and many times retains it for life just being that person. Success is easier when the demand is there.

Those examples point out the needs, necessary changes passing through their natural phases while maintaining their function for a time until some other tendency evolves and transforms again just like the universe has been doing forever; or at least as far as "we" can imagine.

Religious transformation has existed since the beginning of spiritual consciousness. Those dates are still debatably unclear and are being constantly and hesitatingly speculated through a combination of religious conjectures, social scrutiny and scientific analysis.

Religious transformation has ventured differently through privately, anarchically, imperialistically and globally dominated religious institutions for a very long time.

Conventional religion in general has grown and saturated other spiritual beliefs to a point of smothering people to transform away from their archaic and inhibiting rules where their growth has reached over its peak in recent centuries; more now than ever. The "new" transformation "is" moving along while many Christians, Jews and Muslims etc. may not be exercising their privileges of discussing the inevitable transformation because of either being unaware of its momentum, not fully understanding it or from suffering anxieties of losing what they "think" they have similar to how the Jews and Romans felt when Jesus was rising in popularity. The new transformation is on the rise.

There will probably always be those who "hang on" and resist change or differences. Real reality in our spiritual beliefs is a part of our oncoming future and is filled with more meaningful inner strengths than ever before. Let us gain more inner strength for improving our "lives," not living for fantasies of after life or worshipping a nonexisting entity.

The music in churches is getting much louder drowning out the serenity, praying and misconceiving philosophy of old time religious activity. Church activity is losing its prestige with boisterous entertainment. Others are slowly venturing into developing our spiritual strengths within so we can utilize our natural spirituality.

We "are," little by little, gaining new awareness and ability to become healthier on our own merits, not helplessly dependent on a "God" to do it. Many people say, "Let God handle it." This is wishful conjuring and teaches us a faith of fantasy where it isn't necessary to exert energy to acquire something. That's freeloading. This newly adopted spiritual awareness allows us to use that believing power which is within everyone of us in various degrees, not a thing out in space. Once we understand the actuality of this conventional view of God power "within" us, we can, but we no longer have to use the term God. Then it respectfully becomes "our" better than ever mind power to perform "human" feats of wonder, not fallacious miracles of fictitiously supernatural magic; that is, unless one prefers to live in misconception and fantasy as they have been in recent and past time beliefs.

There is no reason for anyone to fear this spiritual transformation moving along as it has been and is continuing. What it does is release dependency on hypothetical god power out there somewhere and places that power within the self. Yes, this "is" a somewhat new spiritual study, concept and practice even though it has always been available and many have used it.

We are transforming or exchanging, if you will, our concepts of a "big man" in space who becomes nonexistent when we say so and believe it. Then we are converting that belief energy into our own selves creating our own security system and confidence of it.

Once again and maybe many times more, we are venturing away from imaginatory figures which are represented by the terms of supernatural, magical, divine, God and the like terms. If we choose, we will always have the free choice of using those terms. That pertains to everyone who chooses to think, feel, understand and believe in the self. We never have to give up what we choose to own.

That power we humans have called God's power in conventional religion has evolved in us inherently and traditionally through the ages probably longer than we were aware of. We humans were only conscious enough of it to give it a title and a position in our lives which made it seem real at the time. Now, we understand it has served its purpose for the obvious intellect we were limited within the past few millenniums.

Now we have been becoming and are ready for branching out with our more developed intellectual abilities and reshaping spiritually to manage these oncoming, passing through and eventual ongoing spiritual ways of our God type power within ourselves.

The term spiritual now has a more developed meaning of being "within the mind" or "spiritual mind" which deals with feeling, thought, desire and belief in the self, not in a God in space as it would seem.

Conforming to or with this or "any" new regime of believing isn't readily necessary. Understanding it and its inevitability is far more meaningful. Time will unveil more knowledge as it transforms through the time of change.

We are now, in this space of time, intellectually ready to move into and along with this religious/ spiritual transformation which is here to stay until other phases of the future unfolds.

Religious spiritual, metaphysical or Buddhistical institutions etc. are "in position" to understand, flow into this transformation and further teach being spiritually responsible for the self. It's here to stay and we will serve ourselves well; all of us.

Chapter 15

Creative spirituality and reality

Moving into and through with religious/spiritual transformation is a time and opportunity to stimulate our creative instincts and either our acquired or acquirable skills with unlimited spiritual possibilities.

"Skills" in believing you ask? Sure, why not? Remember, past religious teaching involved indoctrinating people to do what they were told to do or to not do at the risk of being punished somehow or at the risk of going without something if not conforming, so we need new skills to stay focused on our goals.

Many times, more than not, people have been so emotionally caged up with strict and guilt inflicted influence causing inhibitive religious pressures, they have become quietly or outrightly hostile through bursting anger of being fed up with cooped up restrictions, plus religious societies refraining from openly analyzing those continuously reoccurring pressures "throughout" communities of the world.

Generally, what one can't have, one wants all the more. We are now intelligent enough to handle more spiritual freedom. That means becoming more spiritually and morally stable within through this religious/spiritual transformation and less social and religiously regulated by those pressures which tends to dominate people's consciousness and prevent spiritual power within.

When the masses of people become more efficiently stable within from the transformation, families and governments will follow the forming spiritual practices. They have been overdue for a good length of time. Then we will see the patterns of spiritual conflict diminish and we will mingle peaceably with one another. It's all about believing and being creative within. Then we become better for ourselves and others too.

The following are suggestions for beginning one's transformation from past dependency on conventional religion to self-dependent spirituality. These are not rules! They are suggestions only:

#1 Gain more perspective on and in as many religious denominations as possible.

#2 Gain as many nonreligious views as possible.

#3 Gain exposure to metaphysical practices (religious science, Buddhism and Transcendentalisms etc.). Explore them in as many ways as possible and analyze them rationally for their make sense value or not.

#4 Do not choose any of them too soon in the same way one would not choose a mate too quickly.

#5 Observe and learn the past and present progress of them all.

#6 Decide on which one can be "real."

#7 Be sure one is not based on believing only without analyzing.

Experiencing them all allows a much wider perspective to form a much wiser and self-satisfying resolution for use as one's future unfolds.

Develop creative programming, as one study's perspectively, within the self on a regular bases and be that part as long as it is "not" in fantasy.

Existing in fantasy by means of man-devised religion makes living seem easier while peace and contentment is on the daily agenda and many times when one needs help to get through a tough time etc. What one may need to be aware of is, as mentioned before, the help one does get when praying to God for help so much of the time, if not all the time, is actually the patience and self-spiritual strength which churns in the mind of the self. That "is" spiritual power in believing, not necessarily with any God. Praying to God is praying to and with our spirit within. The verbal term God stimulates our spiritual power within for doing wonders within. It "can" mean our attracting help from outside of us, but only with our effort, not supernaturally as conventional religion professes. Remember, it has to make realistic sense. That's what build's its power within. One has to learn to work with it through practice, determination, patience, belief and "faith" in the self. It all adds up to acquiring more confidence and trust in the self.

This belief of inner self-spirituality is so closely related to and with the concept of divine spirituality. It just isn't connected with a "thing" concept of God out in space or in mystical form. It has to do with God type of power within the self. That must be clearly understood so "no" misunderstanding occurs anywhere between anyone. Let us all think "clearly."

Also remember, this is about reality within ourselves as compared to fantasy in the conventional manner of religion. Religion is a practice and belief of a God out there "somewhere." Spirituality within is a practice and belief of untainted spiritual power within the self (not magical or supernatural).

Chapter 16

Spiritual ownership explained

Are we owned by anyone or by anything? Is anyone or anything owned? Does anyone or anything belong to anyone or anything? These views are only to be inspected for value chosen:

A paid registration states one owns a car. That's only a legal statement which says use it for awhile.

Actually, we cannot own anything. We cannot even own ourselves. We only use ourselves while we are alive. So you think you own what you eat? Guess again. Even all the food and liquid we consume doesn't become of part of us like we might think when we're eating it. Right, it all went down the drain; almost every last bit of it.

How about a business we seem to be so proud of "owning." It's not really ours. We are only putting out energy working on it for awhile. Then it's gone through problems, retirement or merges.

When two become married, they like to think they have become one together; hence own each other. What wonderful security they "think" they have. Some don't care for that ownership in awhile. Some lose their spouse to death and ownership is gone. Some want their own separate lives in marriage without ownership.

Mama says, "I'll always have my baby, even when she grows up." True? Baby grows and is gone at 18. Mama says, "I'll own her kids." Her kids grew fast and out the door as teens. Mama has no one again. Now she's too old and won't even allow a man or anyone else in her life. Even when she died, she couldn't take her paid off house with her. While struggling with ownership, people strive to "keep" what they think they own.

Everything spiritual is psychological. So is ownership. That means we can call it spiritual ownership. It's within our minds. Realizing that gives us spiritual strength; independent spiritual strength while we are alive. Let us be more aware of reality.

Since "God" has been known to run everything in the universe, maybe "He" owns us, right? Wrong! He can't own us if he doesn't really exist! So, is it worth taking a chance on submitting ourselves under "His" ownership if he may not even exist?

Looks like the only thing we will ever own is a spirit of God so many of us like to believe is inside us. Depending on a spiritual entity somewhere "out there" certainly cannot be understood as being owned, but it "is" reasonable to believe in our own God within, if we choose that terminology. It is owned individually by each one of us until our lives are finished. We can also claim that power within is our own creative spirituality with or without any other titled terminology.

Since God is conceived as being everywhere, "He," again if you will, might be so far out in the vast universe, he may not even hear us; that is, if he was really real or at least a something as compared to being nonexistent.

If God was really a being of some kind and controlled everything, "he" probably wouldn't allow these derogatory sounding scripts to be publicized.

What we have, after passing through religious transformation, is pure unadulterated self-creating spirituality without the clutter of misguiding outdated and structural beliefs to upset our manners of believing in ourselves.

Pure spirituality is here to stay. It belongs to us and is as dependable as we are alive.

Material things and us aren't steadily owned. They are only borrowed for awhile. Creative and exchangeable ideas are spiritual. They flow from one person or group to another via communication and reformation. Very few ideas remain the same.

Creative and exchanging ideas and thoughts aren't materialistic or tangible. They are spiritual. Adopting a sense of believing within the self is spiritual. Utilizing the God type power within, not beyond the self, is potent spirituality, once again, within the self and thoroughly controlled by the self.

Once a person understands religious transformation isn't dumping one sense of believing and picking up another, that person can understand the transfer is a psychological concept of spiritually "dealing" with a developing inner strength which was previously and spiritually assumed to be a spiritual image accepted as "God." That means the spiritual responsibility would be assumed or accepted by the individual. Hence, spirit within, not spirit of something else.

Spirituality "is" owned while living when it is solely and primarily accepted as basis for spiritual believing of directing the self. When everyone, with the exception of the mentally handicapped, the very young and possibly cases of dementia, adapting to religious transformation and praying for others will be unnecessary because everyone will possess independent spiritual power for maintaining individual health of mind, body and survival purposes. What more could one ask?

This spiritual philosophy is supportive of the belief where "the strong survive" and now is available for everyone as it always has been without their being aware of it.

Conventional religion may have been needed in the distant past up to recent centuries, but now the level of human consciousness has raised to the point of automatically increasing our ability to be spiritually sustained without spiritual dependency on deteriorating religious beliefs and their outdated standards, rules and expectations.

The transformation of conventional religion cycling into spiritually self-sustaining existence is certainly not the beginning or end of mankind,

God, our Earth or the universe. It is simply part of cycling concepts of which we learn to flow along with as long as it "has" been here to say the very least.

Destiny of the universe, which of course includes our solar system, doesn't consider or cater to mankind's desires, imaginations or any other neurotic idiosyncrasies. Cycling periods of belief and other human expectations, influences or manipulations are no exceptions. We are here on our own and that is good reason to cycle into being independently spiritual as we choose without worrying about things we have no control over.

One last time, the following is for the beneficial essence of the main theme in these scripts:

If we the spiritual individuals choose to use the old time terminology of the word God which "can" represent belief within, this is exercising our freedom to say, think and believe that power of belief is all within us and has nothing to do with "anything" outside our bodies and minds. That is our birthright privilege to adopt and adapt with that self-initiated spirituality and become free to think and believe the way we choose. We also have our birthright to proclaim ownership of living beliefs and confidence which offers us complete control over our well being with the daily practice of outrightly contending and programming these replacements or adding strengths of belief depending on how one exercises one's choice of believing. Generally speaking, one notices more maturity in spirituality when going all the way with a form of belief as compared to mixing religious beliefs with nonreligious beliefs "just in case." This is all based on what and how we choose to believe while we are living our "alive" life on Earth.

Remember, this is about a supposedly admired entity of billions of people over time "who" if you will, could change bad situations to good situations if he was everything as good as his inventors, promoters and supporters have envisioned him to be. If he is uncommunicable, he isn't there and he isn't real. We and our spirituality are and we can do wonders with ourselves without that incommunicable entity or belief.

Your author, Lloyd E. McIlveen unveils a chronological list of many and various book subjects presenting controversial, educational, uplifting, futuristic, self-helping, philosophical, psychological, entertaining and other stimulating concepts of which are and will be displayed with brief descriptions of each book as follows:

1. "Evaluating Outdated Beliefs" This is a report, viewed through the perception of your author of the evolutionary process and changes occurring in belief; especially in the area of religion and spirituality, This was designed for the benefit of broadening individual perception, perspective and viewing "another" plane of belief while revealing fallacies in theological indoctrination. This is an improved revision of the book's origin.

2. "Staying Alive On Planet Earth I" This is a psychology of health required to stabilize and maintain better health for the benefit of living

a much longer life. Source: A lifetime of study, problems, recoveries and many successes more in natural methods.

3. "Understanding Loss To Relieve The Anguish" Loss of anything involves many distractions and disrupting emotional disarray. Gaining greater understanding of these emotions offsets the misery of them and enhances optimism of confidence and support for emotional weakness before, at and during the time of loss.

4. "Understanding Preventing And Eliminating Cancer" presents new views on the wonders of natural methods for practical use.

5. "Paradox Of Progress Unfolding I" This is a tale told by a man "many" centuries into the future about an exciting, overwhelming and terrifying occurrence on planet Earth as a result of their wondrous progress around the time of 2300 A.D. Hang onto your seats! #2 is a second issue later on the list.

6. "Offsetting Climate Change And Nuclear Waste Contamination" This view of the two exposes the hazards, inevitabilities and possible solutions needed now for preventing a "too late" disaster that will affect all living beings too soon.

7. "What God Is And Is Not" This is a study of spiritual possibilities designed, not particularly to remold conventional mannerisms of belief, but to open and expand perception in the most controversial subject of mankind; the subject of God and whether mankind will or won't expand that consciousness along with all progress and growth on Earth and in the universe.

8. "Kids Of The Crick" This is a story of four old fashioned country kids setting out on a weekend adventure in their countryside of tall grass, mountains, rivers, animals, caves and strange living beings. Sometimes, they aren't sure whether it's all real or not.

9. "Paradox Of Destiny Explained" eliminates the mysteries, facades, fantasies and deceptions of how, where, way and when we do what we do and opens new possibilities for expanding our beliefs and consciousness pertaining to this study of available options that may influence insight for growth, change or even justify present mannerisms of what may control the individual, planet Earth or the whole universe and is not zealous, fanatic or bigoted; only assertively revealing.

10. "Paradox Of Progress Unfolding 2" This book is a continued fiction story and can be considered exemplary of "major" human changes that alienated millions of people to another planet in the future. They are led by the elements of unexpected surprises of which is par for the course with gutsy space pioneers. The first "Paradox Of Progress Unfolding I" must be read first to understand and appreciate the

disproportional attitudes and positions of people on a threshold of major change and disasters upon them. This is not only a tale of travel, trials and tribulations, it is philosophically stimulating and adds toward future insightful expansion of the human species.

11. "Staying Alive On Planet Earth 2" This is an extended version of the original psychology of health for living a longer life. More knowledge allows more life.

12. "Preventing The Doom Of Mankind" This is a stimulating, vitalizing and somewhat shocking description of how mankind is "truly" faced with extinction in the "near" future due to their own faults of progress. It's very educational and needed now to help offset that inevitability where the odds dictate we will all perish if we don't adhere to this offsetting of which "is" possible to achieve.

13. "Spiritual Transformation Of The Fourth Millennium" Old-time conventional religion is fading. New-time spirituality is on the rise. Objective realism is the prime issue here for future inclined thinking and believing.

14. "Understanding The Science Of Creative Mind" This is a study for discovering, developing and practicing a psychological powerhouse within for conquering the unconquerable, achieving the impossible or doing things no one has done all depending on, of course, the makeup and determination of the individual. This study brings out a greater potential of the individual's abilities when taken seriously. This was compiled from a lifetime of study and experience from your author.

15. "Living to 150" is a guidance program for intentions of anyone desiring a longer than longer life which is insightfully and innovatively educational for that purpose.

16. "The Act Of Getting One's Act Together" If anyone, business or nation wants to develop their stance, priorities and position in life, this is a chance for them to get their act together more than ever.

17. "Making Changes From This Point Forward" The design of this book is for the purpose of preventing repeated mistakes of unforeseen surprises due to what we weren't or aren't aware of that did, can or will happen again. It's all about gaining or rearranging change consciousness in this area.

18. "Relationships For All" This is a carefully arranged view of how relationships can function much better when initiated or guided by the experiences of many experts and your author who have had failures and successes in their very human encounters. The experiences of more relationships result in wiser judgments and approaches to others.

19. "The We Between Us" helps us in discovering who is good for us and who is not. First it is a study in the book. Then it is a study with people of what exists in two party's minds (individuals business or nations) when first confronted. A real time saver in evaluating possible compatibility or not between the two for anyone. It works.

20. "Passion Of Dance" This is a narrative on progress, value and guidance for the dance inclined. It's informative and inspiring with its history and recent magnetism.

21. "Open That Door" to love. This book is comprehensively all about love. It's not a storybook. It clears up the differences of love that causes misunderstanding, suspicion and deception.

22. "Get The Spirit" This book describes controversial and somewhat intertwined conventional views of spirit, spirits and spirituality. This book

untangles the "usual" views and presents a more perspective manner of living with these concepts of mind.

23. "Stories Of What They Couldn't Or Wouldn't Tell" Ages are from babies to 100 years; twenty four of them.

24. "Improving On Love And Relationships" This one is two books in one. Part one "Open That Door" is a psychology of love that enhances perspective to understand and adapt to a very popular, but deceiving, repressed and ignored emotion; love. Part two covers "Relationships For All" which elaborates on origination, different types, significance, deceptions, desires, experiences, communication, possibilities, future and guidance of relationships. It's comprehensive and also derived from a lifetime of relationship experiences and serious study.

NOTES

NOTES

NOTES

NOTES

NOTES

www.ingramcontent.com/pod-product-compliance
Lightning Source LLC
Chambersburg PA
CBHW030438290526